Talking
Mysteries

Talking Mysteries

A CONVERSATION WITH TONY HILLERMAN

Tony Hillerman
& Ernie Bulow

illustrations by Ernest Franklin

UNIVERSITY OF NEW MEXICO PRESS • ALBUQUERQUE

11 10 09 08 07 06 05 04   1 2 3 4 5 6 7

LIBRARY OF CONGRESS
CATALOGING-IN-PUBLICATION DATA

Hillerman, Tony.
    Talking mysteries : a conversation with
Tony Hillerman / Tony Hillerman and Ernie Bulow ;
illustrations by Ernest Franklin.
        p.   cm.
    Includes bibliographic references.
    ISBN 0-8263-3511-X (alk : paper)
    1. Hillerman, Tony—interviews.
2. Novelists, American—20th century—Interveiws.
3. Detective and mystery stories—Authorship.
4. Navajo Indians in literature.
I. Bulow, Ernie, 1943– .
II. Title.
PS3558.I45Z476   1991
813'.54—dc20   91–2467
                                                        CIP

Map: Deborah Reade
Book design: Jos. Trautwein
Cover illustration & design:
    Kathleen Sparkes

Photo credits ━━
Frontispiece: © Cynthia Farah
pp. 58–61, 122: © Ernie Bulow
p. 120: © Gayle Brown

for Nannette
of course

CONTENTS

HILLERMAN
COUNTRY

INTRODUCTION

Ernie Bulow

In 1970 I was winding up a four-year stint as a teacher for the Bureau of Indian Affairs at Fort Wingate, New Mexico. It had been a mixed experience if there ever was one. Those years were the tail end of the "old" BIA (I've been assured) when most of the teachers and personnel were conservative folk from backwaters of the Bible Belt and Navajo children were still punished for speaking their native language.

The motto of the Bureau was "Let's not work ourselves out of a job," which translates as, "If we do much of a job of educating these kids, they won't need us any more." From the Navajo side there was the magical belief that simply signing up for school each fall equaled an education and regular attendance, homework, and the like were not seen as essential to the process. A Navajo standoff.

The BIA was intent on "mainstreaming" the kids, which meant decent haircuts, shoes and slacks for standard dress, and a generally docile attitude. Schools still had compulsory religious education on Monday nights. During the hours so designated the students were forced from the dorms come wind or snow and expected to attend any one of several fundamentalist brainwashings. If that sounds too harsh for you, picture it from the boys' and girls' point of view. Neither traditional Navajo religion nor the Native American Church were considered religions at the time.

I found myself as alienated from the dominant local culture (using the term lightly) as any of my Navajo students. I wasn't much older than many of them, and it wasn't long before I found myself deeply involved in Navajo life, literature, and religion. For the most part my students and their families were delighted by my interest and happy to share with me. I don't know how many times some Navajo parent said to me, "It's about time some of you teachers came out here to see how we live, find out what we believe in and what we know. You are most welcome."

Over a four-year period I attended and took part in many traditional ceremonies, collected oral literature, and generally immersed myself in Navajo life. With my students I looked into traditional crafts, interviewed old people, stood all night in the biting cold to watch a Fire Dance, promoted high school rodeos, took part in the Native American Church, compiled a book of Navajo taboos that was published by the Navajo Tribe, and generally had a wonderful time.

All the same, by the spring of 1970 I could see my days were numbered with the Bureau of Indian Affairs. Among other things, I refused to shave off my mustache, cut my hair, and quit wearing cowboy boots; never mind how well I taught or got along with my students.

As a voracious reader I generally made do with paperbacks in those days, but an interesting book caught my eye one day. The dust jacket was a striking black, purple, and orange thing with an illustration that was obviously meant to represent a skinwalker or wolfman. It was entitled *The Blessing Way,* by some guy named Tony Hillerman. I read the jacket blurb with some skepticism, but I popped for the five bucks all the same. How we'd all like to go back and buy out the stock at that price.

Sorry to say, the book was a terrible disappointment. I wish it were otherwise. The ethnography of the book was shaky, though some things were only slightly off center. It was something like reading a student paper with a lot of vocabulary freshly mined from a thesaurus. The definitions might be technically all right—by the dictionary— but the usage wasn't quite in register. I didn't know who this Hillerman guy was, but he'd obviously gotten much of his information from books. I was sure he'd never slept in a hogan with fifteen other people or stood in the cold until dawn three nights running to follow an Enemy Way, smelling piñon smoke and feeling the throb of the drum.

Then the mystery itself, so absorbing and suspenseful as it unfolded, petered out with a lame denouement about government secrets and a space shuttle or something. Interestingly, the plot hinges on a "relocation" Navajo, one who learned his culture from a book. Hillerman cites one of the books, a plot device he has used several times since. So I didn't think much of *The Blessing Way* when I first read it twenty years ago, and I forgot about this budding author.

All the same, the book had at least two things going for it, in my opinion. Tony Hillerman, whoever he was, had a hell of a knack as a storyteller. The idea of a Navajo policeman was a winner if I ever saw one. Brian Garfield didn't really make any use of the possibilities at all in his two books about Sam Watchman, *Relentless* and *The Threepersons Hunt*. The Navajo detective was a great idea and opened up a whole world of interesting characters, beautiful landscapes, and a people who see things in different terms than Anglo-American culture.

Of course it didn't matter that in the real world there are no Navajo policemen of the sort Hillerman invoked. In reality they are used primarily as traffic cops and for crowd control at Reservation functions and little else. This is still true today. Crimes of any consequence come under someone else's jurisdiction—county, state, or federal—and any homicide is automatically the province of the FBI.

This has not changed in the twenty years since Hillerman started to write. But the idea is a seductive one and Tony has a plaque from the Navajo tribe to show how they feel about it. They call him a friend of the Navajo because of his respectful attitude toward cultural matters and the dignity with which he invests his Navajo policemen. His novels are used in English classes in Reservation schools and are immensely popular with the Navajo people, being passed from hand to hand until they literally fall apart with the reading.

All the same I was surprised several years later when this same Hillerman won an Edgar award for his third mystery, the second in the Navajo series. I didn't run right out and buy it. I returned to the Reservation in 1974 but things had changed a great deal, thanks mainly to the American Indian Movement, a group never very popular with Indians in the Southwest. Though most Navajos wouldn't have anything to do with AIM—its main appeal was to the disenfranchised—there was still a new tension in Navajo-Anglo relations. It was much more difficult to feel truly comfortable working on a sand painting or acting as Cedar Chief in a Native American Church meeting. The strain was evident at the Hopi villages and at Zuni as well, though I continued to attend as many public dances as possible.

In the course of things I quit teaching and became an Indian trader, dealing mainly in jewelry, kachina dolls, and the odd item. I was still an avid reader, regardless of what other turns my life took, and as a mystery fan I still saw the name of Tony Hillerman about every other year. Big deal, I thought. The jewelry business crashed spectacularly about 1980, and I decided to open a bookstore, the dream of most English teachers who really love their subject matter. Gallup, New Mexico, didn't have a bookstore of any kind at the time, which is hard to believe in a city of twenty thousand people.

To shorten the story, there was this Tony Hillerman character haunting me again. The store did quite well, and I had constant requests for the Leaphorn/Chee books, which Avon thoughtfully kept in print. Many of the requests came from Navajos. The Indian Health Service started an epidemic of its own as Hillerman paperbacks passed from hand to hand until they went through the washing machine in someone's back pocket, fell apart from sheer use, or worse, got stolen by someone who couldn't wait. It was a phenomenon.

Obviously, I thought to myself, this Hillerman must be doing better than that first book I read, or I need to reread *The Blessing Way* and discover what I missed the first time. There was no such thing as a used copy of his books to be had—not even in paper—so I pulled a handful of paperbacks out of stock and set to. Not an unpleasant task, as it turned out. For one thing, the plots had improved. His sense of characterization was sharper, and his use of cultural materials was better and better. He did, however, still have his quota of glitches per book. Some of them—perhaps most—were rather small as I'm the first to admit. Minor details for the most part, which didn't really affect the integrity of the stories at all. These little points weren't bothering his Navajo readers, so why should I care?

Some of the errors were actually pretty funny. In *The Dark Wind* somewhere he has Jim Chee eat a *piki* bread sandwich. Few readers outside the Southwest would give the line a second glance, but for anyone who has ever experienced *piki* the line displays a serious disregard for reality. *Piki* is not a bread, in the first place, despite its name. It is a traditional Hopi food of semireligious significance and is only made on special occasions. On First Mesa, for example, at the village of Walpi, there is a tiny room reserved for its preparation. Ancient griddle-shaped rocks are heated with charcoal, and a thin batter of blue cornmeal is smeared with deft, practiced motion across the hot rock. The resulting product is peeled hastily from the rock and rolled into a scroll-like tube. *Piki* bread resembles a folded roll of very brittle, blue-gray newspaper older than a Dead Sea scroll. At the first bite the whole thing disintegrates into a handful of paper flakes. It actually tastes something like popcorn—sort of. The idea of slapping a chunk of bologna and some mayo between two of these is ludicrous. But not very important, in the end.

In *The Ghostway* Chee takes a sweat bath in his shower by pouring water over hot rocks. The Swedes might approve, but the Navajos never do it this way. The sweat bath is a religious observance—as is virtually all of Navajo life—and the heat is always dry. No water. Ever.*

Then again, hardly any two Navajos will agree on much of anything, and four together will argue until next year about anything at all. While much of Navajo life is formulaic, individual variation is not only tolerated, but encouraged. Hence a lot of confusion. Certainly one of the things Navajos like about Tony's books is the feeling that their secrets are still safe. He doesn't really get into matters of substance for the most part.

What he has is an unerring talent for invoking the mood, using a small bit of culture to weave a convincing tapestry of complex design and intricate pattern. With very little material—actual facts or details—Hillerman can create an atmosphere so absolutely believable it is uncanny. That, I suppose, is the essence of his genius.

Readers usually finish one of his books thinking they have been deeply immersed in Navajo culture, though they have not actually accumulated a lot of factual information. Hillerman's attention to detail and his folksy, oral delivery give readers a sort of conspiratorial charge, as though privy to valuable secrets. And the elements of

AUTHOR'S NOTE: As Ernie says, hardly any two Navajos will agree on much of anything, including sweat baths. Chee's bath produced a torrent of contradictory instructions (even a letter from a Doctor of Anthropology who had done her dissertation on the subject). Chee takes his much as does a Navajo I know up near Red Mesa, except my Red Mesa friend squirts water on his hot stones out of a little Joy detergent bottle. Ernie is right about *piki* bread but may not have noticed that the noun is now being used here and there for a variation of fry bread, much better for baloney sandwiches. As for *The Blessingway*, he is absolutely right. I like some parts of it, but a lot of it makes me flinch.—Tony Hillerman witchcraft and supernatural, given their cultural context, are surefire attention getters. And holders.

So convincing is he that trial lawyers call him for advice. Newspaper and magazine editors hound him for pieces and articles of an overwhelmingly technical nature. The world at large believes he is a walking encyclopedia of Indian lore. He's the first to laugh at such an idea. But he knows how to get a lot of mileage from a bit of information, a scrap of philosophy, a hint of an idea. And he is absolutely true to the spirit of his material. The facts, the tiny details, are relatively unimportant in the face of the significance of a thing. It is important, after all, that Chee eat a *piki* bread sandwich. He's an Indian. He needs to eat Indian food. *Piki* bread certainly sounds tasty enough. It functions for Tony just right.

Soon after I opened the bookstore in 1980 Hillerman gave a reading at the Gallup Public Library. It was a small but devoted crowd that turned out to hear him read from *The Dark Wind*. Almost as soon as he started to read in a voice hinting at his Oklahoma heritage, it was obvious that he didn't know how to pronounce the names of the Hopi villages, Hopi names, or Hopi words that popped up in the text. I wanted to be a bit embarrased for him, but the audience seemed not to notice. As his storyteller's cadence swung into the scene where Jim Chee interviews the old Hopi man I forgot all about pronouncing the names of villages. It was really irrelevant. There isn't much action in that scene, but the old man, and the room, and the interview absolutely came alive. They are as real and absorbing as anything in modern American literature, and far more accessible than most modern fiction.

Another of my favorite scenes comes when Chee has gone to Los Angeles to follow a lead and ends up talking to the old man at the senior citizens' home. Every time the fellow bangs his walker to unjam his tongue I laugh with delight. It is a wonderful scene though the ingredients are common as dirt and sun and grass. No violence, nothing exotic nor erotic—heaven forbid—just a respectful young Navajo willing to listen to an old man nobody else is paying attention to. Wonderful stuff.

After that first meeting in Gallup I got a short note from Tony that asked, "Are you the Ernie Bulow who did the taboo book, and can you get me a copy?" As it happened I had just reprinted the book myself and I sent one off to him. After that I started seeing Tony with some regularity at meetings of writers, gatherings of arty New Mexico folk and the like. Since most folk in New Mexico are arty and gather at the drop of a tortilla chip, the meetings were fairly frequent. Every time I saw Tony I worked on him for a book signing at my store. When I closed up five years later I'd still never had a Hillerman signing. That's the way things happen sometimes.

The other thing we talked about with regular frequency—it must have been monotonous frequency for Tony—was some sort of little publishing project. At the time he had two unpublished stories he'd done for *Playboy*. Though one had appeared in an anthology in Europe, neither had seen print in America. The original idea was to publish the two stories with a covering essay and a biographical sketch of Hillerman by me. Nice idea.

But Tony was getting increasingly popular and *Black Mask* got reproduction rights to one of the texts. Another friend of mine, Dennis McMillan, had just published a limited edition of *The Ghostway* and that seemed like a possibility. During the early years of our association I had found a few rare books for Tony—things he needed for his research. Then gradually I had begun to give him some technical advice and read manuscripts for ethnographic errors—things that were errors according to my light, of course.

I approached him eventually with the idea of letting the stories go—especially as the second one appeared in an anthology called *The Ethnic Detective*. Instead, I would do a limited edition of the book in progress. As the details got worked out, the work in progress shifted from *Skinwalkers,* which was now fait accompli, to *A Thief of Time,* which was just being hatched. As an excuse for the limited edition I had a Navajo friend who loved Hillerman's books, and who could illustrate as a knowledgeable insider, do some drawings from the uncorrected manuscript. At that time Ernest Franklin was busy filling in blank spaces in copies of Tony's books for fun and profit. Only a Navajo could really do justice to the books and show how the terrain, the people, the sky should look. As soon as Hillerman saw some of Ernie's work he was hooked. Franklin did twenty-six black-and-white drawings for *A Thief of Time* before Harper and Row quashed the whole project by deciding to do a limited edition of their own, unillustrated.

While we were working out this latest setback we all got involved with reprinting the *Black Mask* story in a slick new magazine out of Phoenix called *Native Peoples*. Franklin did the story illustrations and "Chee's Witch" saw print again. Tony, by this time, was on the best-seller list and was being approached constantly for talks, signings, and personal appearances of one sort or another. My limited project looked hopeless. Then in the fall of 1988, we decided to do some interviews, add the story that hadn't seen recent publication, the autobiographical essay that complements the interview, and throw in the drawings (you figure out what they illustrate). We titled the result *Words, Weather, and Wolfmen: Conversations with Tony Hillerman.*

I won't go into all the gory details of self-publishing a limited edition book. For lots of reasons I tried to keep the typesetting, printing, and all close to home. Probably a big mistake. Technical problems dogged us from the first. We finally got to press, and I managed to leave the limitation pages on Tony's doorstep like an orphan child a few days before his promotional tour for *Talking God.* Even then I still didn't know half the troubles waiting to be encountered in the printing and binding process. It ended by taking another six months of hair pulling, phone calls, and tons of antacid as pages were lost, copies miscollated, and various bindings and slip cases tried and rejected. The variant books, at least, should be fun for collectors and bibliographers. Louis Hieb's recently published bibliography of Hillerman's works gives *Words, Weather, and Wolfmen* a substantial entry, and he still doesn't have it all correct.

Since then Tony Hillerman has reached the *New York Times* best-seller list with *Talking God* and again with *Coyote Waits,* a book that pleases most readers by returning to the Reservation and traditional Hillerman storytelling. In addition, many mystery buffs are probably unaware that *Skinwalkers* won the Western Writers of America Spur Award for Best Western of 1987. Hillerman continues to be honored, and his legion of loyal fans grows by the day.

Now, the University of New Mexico Press wants to re-title *Words, Weather, and Wolfmen* as *Talking Mysteries* and issue it in a trade edition with significant corrections and additions. Not surprisingly, I think that's a great idea. I hope it serves to introduce the public to the work of a talented Navajo artist who still deserves to be Hillerman's official illustrator. And I think there is some revealing material in the several hours of conversation transcribed pretty much the way it took place. Tony is quite candid here, and I think there is insight into the man as well as the writer.

This is not a "how-to" piece. I think writers like Tony are born and then made, but no amount of hard work will make a writer a great storyteller. That is a talent bestowed by the gods, or at least the muses. Let's hope Tony doesn't get tired of his Navajo characters for years to come.

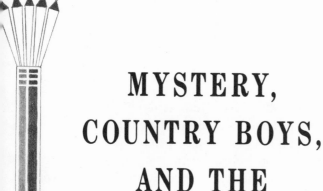

MYSTERY,
COUNTRY BOYS,
AND THE
BIG RESERVATION

✝

Tony Hillerman

Funny how you never rid yourself of the psychological baggage you collect as a child. At about nine, I became aware that two kinds of people make up the world. Them and us—the town boys and the country boys.

The town boys got their hair cut in barber shops, knew how to shoot pool, didn't carry their lunch in sacks, wore belt pants and low-cuts instead of overalls and work shoes, had spending money, knew about calling people on telephones, and were otherwise urbane and sophisticated. We were better rifle shots, better at riding horses, could endure hot hours feeding the hay baler, and, until we tried it, were better at fistfighting. Thus the them-and-us division of my childhood was totally without racial-ethnic lines. Our Seminole and Pottawatomie Indian neighbors were part of Us, fellow barbarians teamed against Them, the town-boy Greeks. My Indian playmates, the Nonis and Harjos and Deloneys, were as sure as I was that the town kids looked down on them, not because they were Indians but because we were all country bumpkins.

I have since become old enough to know the above is mostly nonsense. Konawa, Oklahoma (home of the town boys), with its main street, two banks, drugstore, ice house, theater where a movie was shown every Saturday, and competitive pool halls, wasn't much more urbane than Sacred Heart, Oklahoma, the crossroads with a filling station and cotton gin, which was the center of our country-boy universe. But wisdom about such things doesn't change ingrained attitudes. When I met the Navajos I now so often write about, I recognized kindred spirits. Country boys. More of us. Folks among whom I felt at ease. When I saw them standing around the fringes of a Zuni Shalako ceremonial, dressed in their "going-to-town" velvet and silver but still looking ill at ease, bashful, and very much impressed by the power of the town-boy neighbors, I saw myself, and my kinfolks, and my country friends. That begins explaining why I use a Navajo Tribal Policeman as my Sherlock Holmes, and The People who herd their sheep in the mountains and deserts of the Navajo Reservation as the background of my mystery novels. It is part of the reason I use the culture of The People as the turning point of my plots. But there's more to it than that.

The first Navajos I saw happened to be engaged in an Enemy Way, one of the curing ceremonials The People conduct to bring themselves back into harmony with their universe. It was July, 1945. I was just back from World War II, a very senior private first class with a patch over a damaged eye and a cane to help a gimpy leg. I had a sixty-day convalescent furlough and I found a job (in August, 1945, anyone alive could find a job) driving a truckload of pipe from Oklahoma City to an oil well drilling site north of Crownpoint on the Navajo "checkerboard" Reservation. Suddenly, a party of about twenty Navajo horsemen (and women) emerged from the piñons and crossed the dirt road in front of me. They were wearing ceremonial regalia and the man in front was carrying something tied to a coup stick. These were a far cry from the cotton-chopping, baseball-playing Pottawatomies and Seminoles from my past. I was fascinated. Forty years later, I am still fascinated.

What I had seen was the "stick carrier's" camp of an Enemy Way ceremonial making its ritual delivery of the "scalp" to the camp of the patient. He turned out to be a just-returned serviceman like myself—who was being restored to beauty with his people and cured of the disharmony of exposure to foreign cultures. As it happened, it was the same phase of the same ceremony that I would use to make the plot hold together in my first mystery. But twenty years would pass before that would happen. (In fact, I called the book *Enemy Way,* but Harper and Row decided it would better be called *The Blessing Way,* after another ceremonial that has nothing to do with the book. This sometimes caused folks to buy it as gifts for pious relatives.)

I wouldn't be writing about this interest in Navajos in relation to the mystery novel had not a lot of other circumstances coincided. First, I grew up in a pretelevision culture which was also often too poor to buy batteries to operate the radio. People sat on front porches, or on the benches which lined the front of my dad's general store, and told tales. A lot of value was attached to being good at it. In Sacred Heart, Oklahoma, being a storyteller was a good thing to be.

Second, Sacred Heart had no library. The nearest one was at the county seat, thirty-five miles away. If you loved stories, as I did, you ordered books from the mimeographed catalog of the state library, using a system which guaranteed a broad education. You would order *Captain Blood, Death on Horseback, Tom Swift and His Electric Runabout, Flying Aces,* and *Treasure Island.* A month later a package would arrive. Inside would be a mimeographed letter signed by the librarian:

I regret to inform you that the volumes you request are not on our shelves at this time. I have substituted titles which should meet your needs.

These books would be *History of the Masonic Order in Oklahoma, Horticultural Chemistry, Modern Dairy Management,* a biography of William Jennings Bryan, and the Lord North translation of *Plutarch's Lives of Famous and Illustrious Men of Greece and Rome.* But now and then some chaff would be included amid the grain. When I was about twelve, the package included some of P. C. Wren's foreign legion blood and thunder (*Beau Geste,* I think it was) and a novel about a half-breed Australian aborigine policeman who could solve crimes in the desert Outback because he knew the country and understood the culture. The memory of this strange ethnology and a plot in which the grotesque, empty landscape was as important as any character lingered on. I forgot the name of the book and its author until, thirty years later, a book reviewer reminded me, accurately, that I must have been influenced by the late Arthur Upfield.

I have also been influenced by other suspense and mystery writers, the ones who demonstrated the rich possibilities of the form. Eric Ambler comes first, mostly because he never wrote the same book, or anything like the same book, twice. (For example, *A Coffin for Dimitrios, Passage of Arms, The Light of Day*—totally different, totally successful.) And then Raymond Chandler, at his best a better writer than Ambler, and a master of setting scenes which engage all the senses and linger in the mind. Not as versatile, but better at the sociological end of the game. Reading *The Little Sister* should make anyone aware that the mystery form, applied with craftsmanship and talent, can be literature. Naturally Graham Greene is on the list. How can anyone who wants to be a storyteller read *The Third Man* or *The Comedians* and not feel the urge to try the feat? True, Greene is an artist. But it's the master craftsman in him which builds the mood that makes the books.

I should mention others. The late Ross Macdonald taught every one of us that, given enough skill with metaphorical language, one plot is all you ever need for as many books as you want to write. George V. Higgins keeps pulling me back into *The Digger's Game* and *The Friends of Eddie Coyle,* reminding me how that Brueghel of Dialogue performs his art. And when I notice I'm slipping into those bad habits of adverbs, adjectives, complicated sentences, and turgid prose, I reread my dog-eared editions of E. B. White, or what Hemingway was writing when he was still young enough to care about it, or Joan Didion's superb journalism. When someone has emerged, as Didion had, as American grand master of nonfiction, the National Humanities Council or the MacArthur Foundation, or some such group involved with the betterment of our culture should bribe that person not to waste that talent on fiction.

However, I think I can understand what motivated Didion to take the step. Working with facts, as a journalist must, is like working with marble. Truth has its beauty but it doesn't bend. In the seventeen years I spent covering crime and violence, politics, and that "deviation from the normal," which journalism defines as news, the longing grew to take a vacation from the hard rock and move into the plastic of fiction. Instead of spending a laborious week digging out elusive facts, simply make them up. If you want a rumble of thunder outside the courtroom, then thunder rumbles. If you need a one-legged Navajo to make an ironic remark, you create the Navajo, strike off a leg, and he says exactly what you want him to say.

There's more to it than that. Along with the urge to free yourself from the strictures of fact and the onerous labor of digging data out of files and worming it out of reluctant bureaucrats, there's the headful of material every reporter collects. No job exposes a writer more often to that basic raw material of fiction—people under stress. It accumulates: the woman trying to recapture the logic that led her to kill her sleeping husband and her child, the teenaged boy still smelling of smoke who might have saved his brothers from their burning home, but saved himself instead. The oil company executive who has just lost a bankruptcy battle and with it all he has lived for for most of his life. The man on death row who believes his mother might claim his body and bury it in some private place, if you could only find her for him. The politician who has just lost his temper and shouted into the microphone a truth that he knows will ruin his career. The tense chess game played out in the legislative finance committee. The psychotic desperation of a prison riot. The hungry dream of the anthropology student hoping to prove a thesis in the dust of what was once a Folsom Man hunting camp. The teen-aged sisters in the sheriff's office signing the papers which accuse their father of raping them. All handled in five hundred words or less—or maybe a thousand if you have a loose edition.

Thus at the same time the yen builds to work in something more malleable than hard fact, an urge grows to try to deal with the meaning of all this. For me, it became specifically a desire to write *The Fly on the Wall,* which was going to be my version of the Great American Novel. Trouble was, I was having the problem all newspeople seem to have with that book in the bottom drawer. If you work with words all day at the office, it's tough to work with them at home. Each day you get older with nothing literary to show for it except a few more pages of false starts.

When all this was happening to me, I was thirty-eight. Marie and I had five children and had been living in Santa Fe, where I was editor of *The New Mexican,* for eleven years. We decided it was time for a change. I resigned. We moved to Albuquerque. I enrolled as a graduate student in English at the University of New Mexico and lined up a part-time job as handyman, writer, caddy, doer of undignified political deeds, etc. for the university president.

The terrible moment had arrived. Naked and exposed. Nothing left to hide behind. No more excuses (or grocery money). Either you can write fiction or you can't.

My reasoning went something like this. While I intended, ultimately, to challenge Tolstoy, I wasn't ready to try *War and Peace, American Style.* That would run maybe 250,000 words, a lot for a fellow who has been conditioned to describe the Texas City disaster in a page and a half.

First I would write something shorter, and something with a shape. I would practice on a mystery. I checked a few out of the library, took a look at techniques, counted words on lines, lines on pages, multiplied, and came out with about 80,000. That sounded like the Boston Marathon to a one-hundred-meter dash man, but not impossible. And, since I was uneasy about my ability to plot, but cocksure of my ability to describe, I would play out my tale against an exotic, interesting background, à la Ambler, Greene, et al.

Back to the Navajos. The interest rooted in the 1945 encounter had flourished. United Press had transferred me in 1952 from a job as state capitol reporter in Oklahoma City to manage the two-man Santa Fe bureau. Santa Fe is surrounded by Pueblo tribes, with their complex kachina religion and their secret kiva fraternities. Thus the Indians you get acquainted with there tend to be from the tightly built little pueblos of Santo Domingo, Santa Clara, San Juan, or San Ildefonso. In other words, town boys. Great people, but the country boys were for me. And the country boys were the Navajos, 150,000 of them scattered across their huge complex of reservations in Arizona, New Mexico, and Utah. I would try my hand at a mystery set on the "big" or central reservation. It would involve an anthropologist engaged in a study of Navajo witchcraft beliefs. His research would lead him into an area where my villain was assured privacy for nefarious deeds by pretending to be a skinwalker to scare away the sheepherders.

Now comes the time to outline a plot. Right? Common sense seems to demand it in a mystery novel. I tried. A few chapters into the book it began sounding like nonsense. Tried again. No better. I decided to design a conclusion and outline from both ends toward the middle. It didn't work. Finally I put the outline aside. I would write a first chapter, perhaps even a second one, and grow the outline from that. I wrote a first page, rewrote it, rewrote it five more times. Wrote a second page, etc. Finally finished a first chapter. It was a fine, polished first chapter, made up of nicely honed paragraphs, good sounds, metaphors which fit, etc. I still have it somewhere in a manila folder labeled First Chapter. There are several such first chapters in that folder, each the product of weeks of work and each useless unless I can find a magazine willing to publish a series entitled "First Chapters Abandoned When Their Books Divorced Them." It took me several years to learn the First Chapter Law.

The First Chapter Law is, "Don't spend much time on it. You're going to have to rewrite it." It has proved true for me and I suspect it is true for all of us poor souls who can't draw a blueprint and have to let our stories grow as they go. (If you want to make that disability sound critically respectable, think of Athena growing unplanned from the forehead of Zeus.)

I suspect I had the first inklings of this law about one hundred pages deep into the first book. By then the anthropologist who was the central character had taken on a distinct personality in my mind. (I can see him now, freckles and all.) He was not really the sort of fellow I had intended him to be, less heroic and more academic—the product of the author associating with too many live anthropology professors, I suspect. Another character, an officer of the Navajo Tribal Police whom I had intended to be nothing more than a cardboard device for passing along information to the reader, had also take on three dimensions and was clamoring for a bigger part. Add this to other factors and it was obvious that the wonderful first fourteen pages no longer led into the book I was writing. Out it went, with no more trauma than amputating one's thumb. I wrote a new first chapter which established mood, put the reader into the canyon country, and announced that the game would be Navajo witchcraft.

That short first book required almost three years of spare time, being interrupted by papers about Shakespeare, Chaucer, Milton, and Thurber, a graduate thesis, and the part-time job as presidential handyman. It was also frequently interrupted by moments of sanity. It would occur to me in these periods of lucid reality that no publisher would ever print the stuff I was writing, no one would ever read it, what I was doing was an unconscionable waste of typewriter ribbon. At such times I would put the book on the closet shelf to collect dust until the urge revived itself.

Even at that pace, if the book is short enough you finally finish it. In the case of what came to be *The Blessing Way* this didn't exactly happen. I almost finished it. All that was needed was a final chapter in which justice is done and all questions resolved in an ultimate flurry of exciting action. This eluded me. Finally, sick of the entire project, I tacked on an ending in which the bad guy is shot. I sent it off to my agent.

I had an agent because my master's thesis at the University of New Mexico was a series of experiments in descriptive prose aimed at a popular audience. The chairman of my thesis committee had recommended me to his agent, who had been peddling these efforts to various magazines. I had described my intended novel to said agent and she had advised me not to write it. If you have spent seventeen years learning to write nonfiction, she argued, why switch to fiction, which makes less money and is tougher to sell? My agent was giving me good, honest advice. The answer to that question, of course, isn't logical. It has something to do with the ego of the writer. You can't blame an agent for that.

I waited a month, then I called the agent. Any luck? No. The only editor she had shown it to didn't like it. Neither did the agent. Why not? Well, to be candid, because it was a bad book. It fell between the stools. Not a mystery novel. Not a mainstream novel. Showing it around would do no good for my reputation, nor for hers. What should I do? Come to my senses and go back to nonfiction. Failing that, rewrite it and get rid of all the Indian stuff. I'll think about it, I said. Send it back.

I thought about it. I had just read an article in one of the writer's magazines by Joan Kahn, then the deservedly famed mystery editor of Harper and Row, about the rich possibilities of the form. I wrote Ms. Kahn a two-sentence note. My agent and I disagree about whether I should rewrite a mystery. Would she be willing to read it and settle the argument? I got an immediate one-sentence reply. Send it in.

Those who have seen Joan Kahn's desk—or I should say the mountains of manuscripts under which one presumes there must be a desk—will have trouble believing the following. Only eleven days later I went to Amherst, Massachusetts, to visit my oldest daughter at the University of Massachusetts. On the way back through New York I called Ms. Kahn. Had she found time to read my book? Yes. Hadn't I received her letter? I told her I had been away from home. We want to publish it, she said, if you'll write a better last chapter.

At this state of the game, I learned something new about writing. The MS was no longer merely a box full of typed-upon paper. It was an incipient BOOK. Everything was suddenly easier. Gone was the notion that this was wasted time, that I was only indulging myself. Someone out there was going to receive the message I was encoding. I found myself back in the familiar, comfortable world of the professional writer. I had in my hands a thousand-word analysis from a famous editor, full of shrewd questions and suggestions. I reread the MS carefully. The Navajo Tribal Policeman needed a bigger role to give the book its shape. I wrote a better last chapter (easy when the original is genuinely lousy), beefed up Lieutenant Joe Leaphorn's lines here and there, and inserted an entire new chapter involving only Leaphorn and a nameless horse. Finished! The next one should be easier. And in many ways it was.

For me, writing fiction requires intense, and exhausting, concentration. It's much easier to maintain that with some real hope of publication. *The Blessing Way* provided that confidence. It was a finalist for the Mystery Writers of America best first novel award, losing to *The Anderson Tapes,* a better book. Warner Brothers optioned film rights, Dell bought the paperback rights, and it was well reviewed. Trouble was, my scheme was to make the next book, *The Fly on the Wall,* more a novel of character than a tale of action. Unlike *The Blessing Way,* or any of the books I've finished since, I had a pretty fair grasp of the plot of this one before I started—or at least I thought I did. But when I got into it, I found my storytelling instincts at war with my urge to give the reader a truly realistic view of the professional life of a political reporter. If I stuck to the grand scheme I started with, the story was slowed. To keep the narrative moving, I had to cut out the details needed to give it that DEEPER MEANING that writers talk about after they anoint themselves with the sacred oil of art.

I will always have ambiguous feelings about *Fly.* It fell far short of what I intended. And, despite generally good reviews, it didn't sell well. But it is still a favorite. I wrote it from the single viewpoint of John Cotton, an introverted political reporter. I was totally comfortable in John Cotton's mind, prowling a state capitol as familiar as the palm of my hand and dealing with people I know as well as my own family. I modeled the capitol after the domeless monstrosity in Oklahoma City, but it might have been Jefferson City, or Austin, or a dozen other places which used the same floor plan. The highway contracting scam on which the plot turns was something like one used in New Mexico (and, I understand, in Indiana, Florida, Oklahoma, and wherever politicians build highways). And the investigative techniques used by Cotton are simply a description of techniques I had used to dig through records (a technique made obsolete by computer filing). Yet comfortable as I was with Cotton, even before I finished that book I was yearning to get back to the Navajo Reservation and back to

Navajo Tribal Policeman Joe Leaphorn.

I mean "get back to the Navajo Reservation" almost literally. I love the place—as big as all New England, a landscape of fantastic variety, a land, as someone said, "of room enough, and time." I need only drive west from Shiprock and into that great emptiness to feel my spirit lift. And writing about it gives me the excuse to go.

For some reason which has never seemed sensible in fiction, I seem to need to sort of memorize the places in which my plots take place. For *The Fly on the Wall,* I had driven back to Oklahoma City and prowled the echoing old corridors of the Statehouse to refresh the memories collected in my reporting days. When I was writing *Blessing,* I climbed down into Canyon de Chelly, puddled around on its quicksandy bottom, and collected a headful of sensory impressions (the way the wind sounds down there, the nature of echoes, the smell of sage and wet sand, how the sky looks atop a tunnel of stone, the booming of thunder bouncing from one cliff to another). I seem to write in scenes, and to get the job done I need to remember the details of the stage settings—even though I may use only a few of them.

The way I put a book together, as a matter of fact, sounds on the surface like an argument for writing as a way of life. It provides a professional excuse for daydreaming—that most joyful of all pastimes.

While I always begin books without really knowing where they're going, I never begin a chapter without a detailed and exact vision of the place it will happen, the nature of the actors in the scene, the mood of the protagonist, the temperature, direction of the breeze, the aromas it carries, time of day, the way the light falls, the cloud formations. In other words, I need literally everything imaginable to be in place in my mind. Given that need, the question of "when do you write" becomes hard to answer. I write, at this stage of writing, while driving to the University in the morning. (So far, I have been able to talk the traffic policemen into giving me only warning tickets for rolling through the red lights that this kind of writing risks.) I write during those endless committee meetings which being a university professor entails. I write at cocktail parties, at the cost of sometimes nodding at the wrong time. I write in bed in that period of relaxation at the edge of sleep. Most of all, I do this creating of scenes while sprawled, apparently comatose, on an old sofa in our living room, or sitting on said sofa playing a solitaire game called Spider, which requires two decks but no imagination. Thus it is absolutely impossible to tell whether I am writing or loafing. My wife always gives me the benefit of the doubt.

It sometimes takes a long time to get the scene right by this process, but once it is there, correctly in place, the putting it on paper (more correctly, onto a word processor disc) is fast. The old reporter's conditioning comes to the fore. One simply describes what his imagination has created. Not much rewriting is required.

I do relatively little rewriting in the usual sense. My habit has always been not to leave a page until I have it the way I want it. The revision is done as I go along. I write a sentence, look at it, and usually decide it's okay. If it's not, I tinker, I delete the adverb (repeat one thousand times: using an adverb means you didn't find the right verb. Using an adjective means you need a different noun), reverse the clauses, get it out of the passive voice, fiddle around until it's right. If it's dialogue, I listen to it in my mind. Does it sound like this fat, short-winded, semiliterate fellow talking to a man for whom he has little respect? Right cadence? Suitably incoherent for the spoken word? And so forth. Takes time, but when I leave a page it's finished. There's one huge exception. I know from the outset that I'll come back to chapter one and to other early chapters, to insert material and revise conversations. It's an unfortunate product of writing them without blueprints.

I begin with a thematic idea. For example, in *The Dark Wind* I wanted to expose Tribal Policeman Jim Chee to a crime motivated by revenge—a white value which has no counterpart in the Navajo culture and which seems strange indeed to a traditional member of the Dine'. In *Dance Hall of the Dead,* I was interested in doing something with child-parent relationships. In *Listening Woman,* I hoped to take the Navajo mythology concerning the Hero Twins, and the dichotomy of human nature reflected in the myth, and play it out with a set of orphaned Navajo twins who have their own contrasting notions of heroism. As anyone who has read any of those books needs not be told, I tend to fall short of the original intention. But suspecting that I won't get it all done hasn't made my starting goals any less grandiose. Along with a theme, I invariably begin with a location or two—places on the Reservation where the action will take place, the Navajo Tribal Police substation from which my Sherlock Holmes will be working, etc. This gives me an excuse to go out and nose around, look things over, breathe the air, and talk to The People. This is an opportunity, too, to check the validity of any cultural details I intend to use. Has a tradition I intend to use survived in the part of the Reservation I intend to write about? (A subplot in *The Ghostway* involved Navajo avoidance of buildings in which persons have died. But would drunks avoid a favorite bar because of this? Anthropologists said yes. A Navajo policeman said no. I asked a schoolteacher at Round Rock. He had his class of Navajo teenagers write a paper on the question. The verdict was unanimous. None of the kids would go into that bar. But those who drank had given up the Navajo Way and the teachings of the Holy People. The call of whisky would overpower the voice of the *yeis*. They would ignore the taboo. So, I had to replace the subplot.) I also usually begin with two or three characters in mind. One, of course, is the policeman-protagonist, Leaphorn if I want the older, more sophisticated fellow more comfortable with white ways, Chee if I need the younger, more traditional cop who is still curious about the dominant American culture. Oddly enough, others tend to be victims or secondary folks and not the villain. More than once, in fact, villains have changed identities in mid-book. In *Dance Hall of the Dead*, for example, the graduate-student anthropologist I had intended to be the murderer took on such indecisive, Hamlet-like qualities that I knew he wouldn't have the stomach for it. I changed the plot. Finally, I have in mind some aspect or other of the Navajo culture, and usually several, on which the story will be hung. These tend to be, indeed need to be, the sort of things which Leaphorn or Chee would know about and understand, but which would have no meaning to the Federal Bureau of Investigation, which has jurisdiction in my books—not because of any admiration I might have for the FBI, but because the FBI handles felonies committed on Indian reservations. (My attitude toward the FBI was learned from the working cops one comes to know as a police reporter, which ranged from disrespectful to contemptuous, and from my own observations of the agency during the J. Edgar Hoover days when attention seemed focused on keeping the vest properly buttoned and the hair properly combed. Since Hoover's time, the agency must surely be better than I remember it.)

The next step is to decide where, in the chronology of the story, the first chapter should begin. The first chapter of *The Ghostway* began in East Hollywood about thirty seconds before the victim-to-be became aware that he was marked for a killing. It proved to be exciting, full of tension, etc., but it joined my thick file of first chapters that didn't make it because it bent the book out of shape. The second first chapter began in the Chuska Mountains four days after the victim had been zapped. Wrong again. The ultimate first chapter, very short, opens at a laundry on the Reservation, about three minutes before the victim becomes a victim. I'm never sure how such intangibles are measured, but it seems to be right. It seems to me that the active part of the story should occupy as few days as possible. That requires flashbacks, or those conversations in which character A explains to character B what happened last autumn. I never mind reading those, and I don't mind writing them.

What I do mind is footnotes. It seems to me that I am writing what Graham Greene called "entertainments." My readers are buying a mystery, not a tome of anthropology. Therefore, my first priority must be to keep the story moving. The rule I force myself to follow is that any ethnographic material I work in must be germane to the plot. No fair digressing into marriage customs of the Dine', or the way the sexes were separated in the emergence myth, or the penalties for violating the incest taboo, unless it fits. I have no license to teach anthropology, having simply accumulated what I know through thirty-odd years of making friends, being curious, prowling around the various reservations, and reading what the anthropologists have written. In the second place, the name of the game is telling stories: no educational digressions allowed.

It's not a hard rule to follow. For example, in *Listening Woman* the motive for the murder of Hosteen Tso is to keep the old man from revealing the location of a cave being used by the bad fellows. It opens with Tso being interviewed by a Listener, one of that order of Navajo shaman who diagnoses the cause of an illness, determines what taboo violations have caused the patient to slip out of "hozro" into the disharmony of illness, and recommends which of the scores of curing ceremonials is needed. That done, a singer is called in to perform the proper ritual cure. Tso's responses to the shaman's questions lead the reader through a lot of information about the taboo and curing sickness. But they also provide the information which, while useless to the white folks in the FBI, is illuminating to my Navajo cop. To wit, late in the book I have Leaphorn sitting at the point where the canyon he has been following intersects with a larger canyon. His problem is to decide, in the gathering darkness, whether the place Old Man Tso got into trouble is up the big canyon, or down it. His problem is my problem. A toss-up. I could have him guess wrong and find something to identify his error. Or guess right. I don't like either solution, and neither would most readers. Here's a place for some Navajo logic, for which Leaphorn's Red Forehead clan is noted. I ponder. I go for a walk. What do I know about the Navajo culture that would tell him something useful? Changing Woman, Talking God, and the other *yei* supernaturals taught the first four Dine' clans the Navajo Way, gave them a thousand taboos, including bans against killing most of the forms of life which emerged with them from the final underworld. One of those was First Frog. Killing a frog induces crippling illnesses. I skip back to that much-revised first chapter and insert the following:

"I forgot to tell you," Tso said. "On the same day the sand paintings got ruined, I killed a frog."

I have the old man report that it happened when he dislodged a boulder, and include a few words of internal monologue on the part of the shaman illuminating the seriousness of this.

Now back to page 142, where Leaphorn has been sitting on his rock for about a week awaiting inspiration:

"From his left, from down the dark canyon, came a faint rhythm of sound. Frogs greeting the summer night."

Since frogs are as rare as rich folks on the Navajo Reservation (where rainfall averages maybe eight inches a year), Leaphorn has heard a telltale sound. The reader has learned about the frog taboo, which may be useful to him someday if he plays Trivial Pursuit.

That same first chapter provides probably the best example I can think of when my writing friends try to save me from my slovenly ways and convert me to advance planning. I tried to plan that book. I had five chapters outlined before I bogged down in indecision. I decided I'd begin writing in the hope that this process would light my way deeper into the plot. I wrote the usual misfit first chapter, one of the best ones in my manila folder. Then I revised the outline and wrote a proper one which established the mood, the isolation of the Navajo Mountain canyon country, introduced the character of Listening Woman, and roughed in the dialogue which would be essential to the plot. I reread it. Neat, efficient, and dullsville. It lacked a hook—some interesting action. My outline called for Chapter Two to open a month later, after Hosteen Tso has been murdered. I could solve the dullness problem by having the killer show up in Chapter One and do the dastardly deed. But then he would either also kill Listening Woman, leaving no witness, or he wouldn't, leaving a witness who would tell the cops and convert my novel into a short story. I recalled that the mother of one of my Navajo friends had glaucoma. That disease and resulting blindness is a major Reservation health problem. Why not blind the shaman? Then how do I get her to this isolated hogan deep in the almost roadless country? Create a niece, an intern-shaman, a Tuba City high school girl who drives her auntie around. Kill off niece as well as patient while the shaman is in a quiet place doing her diagnostic trance. Then how do I get my stranded blind shaman back to Tuba City? I'll solve that problem later.

And so Chapter One is remodeled, bearing small resemblance to the outline. Same thing happens in Chapter Two. Introducing Joe Leaphorn alone in his patrol car in the early evening darkness proves too heavy on internal monologue. Insert handcuffed young thief/jail escapee into the front seat for conversation. Leaphorn stops the speeding vehicle of Gruesome George as outlined. As he approaches car to give ticket (as outlined) he glances at bad guy through the windshield, and since I'll need a label for this nameless villain, notices gold-rimmed glasses (as outlined). Here fatigue, whimsy, or inspiration interferes. Why not have Leaphorn see another set of eyes reflecting red from the police car emergency light? Why not, just to be different, put them in the back seat, causing Leaphorn (and the reader) to wonder why? So the eyes are written in, peering out of the back seat. If they aren't useful, eyes are easy to extract—especially on a word processor.

Next chapter. Well, why would someone be sitting in the back seat of this sedan? How about having Gruesome George hauling a dog? A big dog? A huge, trained attack dog? It gives me a way to add something to the villain's biography. It also offers other possibilities, since belief in "skinwalkers" who can change themselves from human to dog/wolf/werewolf is alive and well on the Reservation. Besides, in my earlier life as a reporter I did a feature once on training guard dogs and have a headful of otherwise useless information. And so, a dog (totally unoutlined and unintended) enters the cast of characters in *Listening Woman* and quickly becomes an ingredient essential to the plot. Later in the plot when I'm stuck for an angle, the rearrested thief also becomes useful again.

This business of having knowledge of how to train guard dogs and all sorts of other remembered material on instant recall behind the forehead has been continually useful. The Folsom Man dig site in *Dance Hall of the Dead* I first described as a profile article on a magazine assignment. The endless and self-delusive search for his mother conducted by the bent killer in *People of Darkness* was based upon a young man I interviewed the afternoon before he went to the gas chamber—willing to talk because of an obsessive desire to be buried in a family graveyard somewhere. The former magician, and the card trick so useful in *The Dark Wind,* goes back to an interview with a private detective. I wanted him to talk about detecting. He wanted to talk about his days with the carnival, making a living fooling people with "inertia of the mind." In the same book, the ancient Hopi survivor from the Fog Clan was based on a magazine interview with an ancient member of the Hopi One Horn Society. Again, in *Dark Wind,* recapturing the numbing ambience within a maximum security prison is easy enough if you've spent some time covering the riots, executions, and parole board meetings on the inside. Creating such stuff from go is possible, but it's tough if you are striving for reality.

And I am striving for exactly that. I augment my memory with a copy of that wonderfully accurate and detailed "Indian Country" road map of the Automobile Club of Southern California. I cross-examine my Navajo friends and hang shamelessly around trading posts, police substations, rodeos, rug auctions, and sheep dippings. Good reviews delight me when I get them, but I am far more delighted by being voted the most popular author by the students of St. Catherine Indian School, and even more by middle-aged Navajos who tell me reading my mysteries revived their children's interest in the Navajo Way.

The best review 1 ever received was from a Navajo librarian with whom I was discussing the work of Indian novelists Leslie Silko (*Ceremony*), James Welch (*Winter in the Blood*), and Scott Momaday (*The House Made of Dawn*). "They are artists," I said. "I am a storyteller."

"Yes," she said. "We read them and their books are beautiful. We say, 'Yes, this is us. This is reality.' But it leaves us sad, with no hope. We read of Jim Chee, and Joe Leaphorn, and Old Man Tso and Margaret Cigaret, and the Tsossies and Begays and again we say, 'Yes, this is us. But now we win.' Like the stories our grandmother used to tell us, they make us feel good about being Navajos."

As a fellow country boy, I am proud of that.

A
CONVERSATION
WITH
TONY HILLERMAN

Ernie Bulow

Ernie Bulow: I know that *The Blessing Way* was your first published novel. Was that the first mystery you wrote?

Tony Hillerman: It was the first novel that I had written, yes.

EB: When did you start it?

TH: I don't remember exactly, but it must have been about 1968.

EB: It was published in 1970?

TH: Yes. I might have started it in 1967. I would work on it awhile, and then I'd decide I was wasting my time. I didn't have any time to waste because I was trying to support a family and I was going to school, I was working part-time and I was trying to make a little money on the side writing magazine pieces. So then I would set the novel aside and it would sit there on the shelf for a month or two.

EB: At that time you were teaching in the University of New Mexico journalism department?

TH: I was teaching in the journalism department. I must've started that the same time I first began the book, making false starts at first chapters that didn't lead anywhere. Great, perfectly crafted first chapters, see, that just died.

EB: So, it took something like five years to write.

TH: Yes, but of course you understand there were long periods—months at a time—when I wouldn't be doing anything with it. It would just be sitting there.

EB: How did you find Joan Kahn?

TH: I sent the book to my agent who didn't like it and let me know that she didn't like it and told me it couldn't be published—should be forgotten, abandoned, and that I should get back to writing nonfiction. I didn't want to do that.

As luck would have it, I had read very shortly before that an article in a writer's magazine written by Joan Kahn, who was explaining her theory of the mystery novel and all the things you could do with it. And it didn't have to be this ritualistic, formalized tale of detection—it could be a novel—and you could develop real characters and ideas. Anyway, I approved of what she said. She elaborated what I believed to be true, and she explained the things that had lured me into the mystery field anyway.

I had been reading people like Chandler and Eric Ambler and Graham Greene and the people who had done just what she was talking about. They took the mystery form and made a novel out of it and ground whatever axe they wanted to grind. So, I wrote Joan Kahn a very short letter and asked her if she would read this manuscript, and she wrote me an even shorter letter back—about four words— saying yes, send it in, and I sent it to her.

About eleven days later I was going through New York, and I called her to see if she'd had time to read it yet, feeling rather silly when I did because I didn't see how she could have had time, and she said, "Yes, haven't you gotten my letter?" And I said, "No." And she said, "Well, we want to publish it."

Well, I was totally delighted. When I got home, there was a two-page letter there waiting for me telling me all the things wrong with the book, which is typical of Joan, who is a real professional. Anyway, that's how the first book got published.

EB: How long was it between the first two books?

TH: Only about a year.

EB: Since then, you've sort of been on schedule, if that's the right way to put it.

TH: Yeah, since then it's been about a year-and-a-half between books. If you count the nonfiction, the coffee-table books and that sort of stuff it's been about one book every fourteen months maybe, and then I'd write a little bit of magazine stuff in between.

EB: How thoroughly do you plot in advance and outline your books before you start to write?

TH: Very little, Ernie. I spent a lot of time when I began this business, trying to outline books because common sense tells you that you should, and I think a lot of people who write plotted books do outline them carefully before they start. I've never been able to think that far ahead and now I've reached a point where I think it's probably better not to—in my case anyway—because as I get into a book things begin happening in my imagination that I would never think of in the process of writing an outline or, at least, I *don't* think of when I'm trying to write an outline.

I'll give you an example. In the book called *Listening Woman,* I tried to outline—outlined three chapters and then I bogged down, and I simply couldn't seem to think of where I was going with it. So I thought, "I'll just start writing."

I knew what I wanted in the first chapter. I had, you know, that outline. Two people, the shaman, the woman, the "listener"—except I had her as a hand trembler—and the old man who's going to be a murder victim, who's sick. They were going to have a talk, and I'm describing what he can see through the windshield with the blinker light flashing across it. And I think, well, you won't know this man's name for a long time—until the end of the book, practically. So I've got to tag him so I have something to call him, some way to identify him, so I have him wear gold-rimmed glasses. I'll have Leaphorn see the light reflecting off these gold-rimmed glasses.

Okay, now, time to quit for the night. I'm describing what he's seeing in the dark then—just for the hell of it—I have him see another pair of eyes in the back seat, see. Stick it in there. Clause at the end of a sentence. Hit the period. Turn off the word processor. Go to bed. And I don't know what I'm thinking—I do it kind of whimsically. I don't have any idea why the hell anybody would be riding in the back seat or who that other person is, but I think, you know, I'll just take him out if I can't make him work. And so several days pass before I get back to the book.

I look at where I stopped and I see the extra pair of eyes and I'm thinking, who'd be riding in the back of this car in the middle of the night? What can I do with that? Just take them out? I think, man, another human wouldn't be riding in the back seat. He's carrying, hauling a dog, a big dog. Got to have a background for him, anyway. I'll make the bad guy a dog trainer, you know. He's worked at a—for a veterinarian or something, see. Stole the guy's dog—big guard dog. So I leave the dog in. I leave the eyes in the back seat. Finish the chapter. Write another chapter. By the time I reach chapter four, I am already seeing how badly I need that dog.

EB: Yeah. The dog turns out to be very important.

TH: The dog turns out to be critically important in keeping up tension in the book. I never would have thought of that dog when I was outlining the book. Never.

EB: You just needed a pair of eyes in the back seat. That's how the dog came about.

TH: Well, I just whimsically put him in.

EB: So much for careful plotting.

TH: So much for trying to plan a book in advance. I tried to outline *Dark Wind* a little. Worked on it, wrote a draft of it, a lot of a draft of it. It just wasn't working at all. My wife was conscious that I was having a lot of trouble with the book, and she said, "When you have trouble, sometimes when you go out to the Reservation and spend some time out there, it helps." So I said, "Okay, I'll go." It was winter. It was getting about like it is today. It was late November, early December. Marie said, "I'll go with you, if you want me to," and I said, "Fine."

We had this old Datsun pickup and away we went. She said, "Shouldn't we make reservations?" I said, "Ah, this time of year, there's nobody out there. We'll stay at the Holiday Inn at Kayenta. We get out there to Kayenta and it's almost dark—getting dark—and they're making a miserable western movie out there. So the Holiday Inn is full and so is everything else in Kayenta, which isn't much of a town. By now, it was starting to snow—blowing snow out of the northwest. We drive on and I say, "We'll stop at Coal Mine. Used to be a motel there."

Well, it was there but nobody was home. So we drive on to Tuba City. Motel was there; nobody would come and answer the door. By now, its late, you know, so we sleep out in the front seat of that Datsun in the blowing snow. But that's beside the point.

We drove on to the Hopi Reservation the next day, hopeful of finding a room there at the culture center because we didn't want to sleep in the truck again.

EB: You already knew you were using Hopi as a locale in *Dark Wind*?

TH: I already had the story set on the margin of the Hopi—on the Joint Use Area. My problem was, I didn't have any reason for Jim Chee to be where he had to be.

EB: Among other things he wouldn't have jurisdiction on Hopi land.

TH: No, of course not. He wouldn't. And it was always kind of a glued together improbable situation. So while we're at Second Mesa, somebody vandalized a windmill, believe it or not, and there was a little piece about it in the Hopi weekly. And on the way, I read it and it seemed strange to me that anybody would vandalize a windmill anywhere, but especially in the desert country.

Before we left the Hopi Reservation, I could already see how I had to rewrite the book and how the windmill was going to be the linchpin that held the whole book together because it gave Leaphorn a reason to be where he had to be. It also, later on—though I didn't think of this when I started to rewrite—it gave me a way to develop a climax with the old Hopi. The old Hopi who was the guardian of the shrine.

EB: Now, the old Hopi was somebody whom you'd met in the course of your journalistic activities some years before?

TH: Yes, I do quite a bit of that. One tries to limit the work one makes his imagination do, and here's a good example of where material comes from. Years earlier, *Arizona Highways* had got me to do a story on the Hopi migration mythology, and I'd gone to the Hopi Reservation and talked to people there and set up an interview with this old fellow who was 106 or so—incredibly old, and in one of the kivas—in one of the kachina societies and a member of the One Horn Society, as I recall.

Anyway, he had an interpreter—the Hopi Tribe provided an interpreter—and we talked, and we talked in a room very much like the one I describe in that book. And the old man was carding wool while we talked, as I recall, and it hung in my mind, the whole scene, and I needed something like that, and there it was, ready made. Instead of trying to imagine something, I just remembered it.

EB: It is a favorite scene of mine. Extremely vivid and real. So all you had to add was just the new dialogue?

TH: Changed the dialogue; added the albino boy, you know, a few things like that.

EB: So quite a bit of the material in your books comes from the experiences you have had out there. I mean, it's not all just imagined and intangible?

TH: Quite—as much as I can. I'm naturally sort of lazy. In *Dance Hall of the Dead* that section where Joe Leaphorn approaches the Folsom Man dig with this graduate student is a rewrite from my memory of a story I was commissioned to write years ago for a magazine.

I was asked to do a profile of an anthropological dig, and I picked a Folsom Man site which was being dug by one man, and I spent some time with him, and I simply wrote the same thing I wrote for the magazine. I just described what I saw with this guy digging, you know, changed the conversation, changed the location of the dig, and put it where I needed it to be.

EB: Now, you've used Hopi once and Zuni once, but you didn't really set out with the idea of using each of the Indian tribes of the Southwest in a book.

TH: Oh, no.

EB: But at this point, are you thinking of using, say, Apaches or Paiutes or some other tribe?

TH: You know, what I'm writing now has a subplot involving one of the Rio Grande pueblos. But I'm not going to name the pueblo because of the nature of the book and the nature of what I have going on is a political combat inside the pueblo, see.

The reader just barely gets a glimpse of it, but it's the sort of thing that is kind of negative, and since it is, I'm just simply going to call it "Tano" or, you know, give it a generic

Pueblo name and not make it any one of the real villages. But I doubt if I'll ever base a book—another book—on any of the pueblos.

EB: Well, there are still a number of tribes that have connections with the Navajos. There are a lot of Paiutes in southern Utah and northern Arizona that have coexisted there with the Navajos all this time and they don't get much attention compared to, say, the conflict between the Navajos and the Hopis. So there are groups you haven't used.

TH: These are groups that I know awfully little about, too. Unfortunately. The Utes for example. There's a big old Ute tribe right next door, traditional enemies of the Navajo, and the two still don't get along very well.

EB: That enmity would be something handy you could use to develop a story.

TH: Handy, yes, and it would make sense. But on the other hand, it means I've got to do an awful lot of research on the Utes, which I'd just as soon not do, see.

EB: Do the Utes do bingo?

TH: Probably. I don't know.

EB: I was just thinking, there's an incredible amount of money in bingo on the reservations around here.

TH: Money pours into the bingo games.

EB: Bingo is big business and so obviously that would be a good thing to use for a mystery plot. I mean, you're talking millions of dollars in some instances.

TH: All kinds of things you could do with that. You could have an abortive robbery attempt on a bingo parlor in which some people are killed, for example. Or you could have a lot of missing money to hunt for.

I'm often asked if I'm going to use what happened yesterday, and I always say, "No, no. I don't like to get into fresh, new stuff." But by the time I get to it, it's not fresh, new stuff anymore, and I've thought about how to use it.

The murder of these two Navajos—policemen—near Monument Valley keeps coming up.* And then there's a couple of other strange coincidences. We've had this skinwalker thing.

EB: The one in Flagstaff?

TH: The one in Flagstaff.† And I've heard of another one since then. You know, I don't know what my next book will be about. Usually, about the time I'm getting close to finishing a book, I have the next book nagging at me to get written.

EB: Now one thing that seems to be very easy for you is plotting.

TH: Oh God, Ernie, the only thing that's terribly difficult for me is plotting.

EB: Oh really? That seems to be sort of your strong suit. The descriptions of places and things seem to come easily too, but your plots are so natural and convincing—at least since *Blessing Way*. What I'm building up to is that one of the things that people are fond of saying is that your plots are right out of the headlines, the stuff we were just talking about. And of course your background is journalism, so it's not really surprising that you would like topical subjects.

*The Monument Valley incident involved the murder of two Navajo policemen. The case was sensationalized because the dead men and their police vans were moved some distance and then set on fire. In many ways this seemed like un-Navajo behavior, especially since traditional Navajos will do almost anything to avoid a corpse. Four Navajo men were eventually indicted for the murders, which may have resulted from some sort of drinking spree. Three of them were convicted.

†The Flagstaff trial that spawned the term "Wolfman Defense" involved a man who allegedly murdered his wife because she was a witch. The argument ran that since she was a figure of evil the husband couldn't help destroying her, therefore it should be seen as an act of self-defense. Defense lawyers tried to involve Hillerman as an expert witness. He declined, but his name popped up in various news articles. The man was convicted of murder, though a traditional Navajo jury probably would have acquitted.

TH: Well, it's very important to me that the stories seem realistic. They seem about people who could really *be* people and things that could really happen. I'm writing about the reality, and frequently the headlines happen after the book is started, or long finished.

EB: That's been especially true lately. I had a clipping that I forgot to bring you, that appeared recently in Gallup about that trial in Flagstaff where they began to refer to the defense as the "skinwalker" defense, and your name came up repeatedly as though you had invented the whole thing. How did you feel about that?

TH: I felt really sort of silly. I didn't even know that that had happened, but I did get telephone calls from attorneys involved in the case asking me about witchcraft, and I sicked 'em onto people who know more about that than I do, and I gather they were in communication with those people. And then I had the same thing happen in another way about the case up near Monument Valley that was finally tried in Salt Lake City about the murder of the two police officers.

EB: The headlines appearing in the Gallup and Farmington papers mentioned the name of Tony Hillerman as though he were responsible for the whole incident, like a copycat crime. I suppose that's publicity you could do without.

TH: They treat me as if I were the guru of witches around here. I had calls from reporters in Salt Lake City and Gallup and Farmington and a couple of other papers all wanting me to discuss some witchcraft aspects of the case. I was perfectly willing to do that, given the fact that I know something about the subject, but I'm no world-class authority on Navajo witches. A lot of people know more than I do about the subject. I'm just interested in it, and one tends to collect knowledge or what you assume to be knowledge.

EB: I have been reading your books since the first one was published. I was living in Fort Wingate then and interested in anything to do with Navajos. One of the things I have followed with interest in your books over the years, besides their obvious topical interest, which we've been discussing, is the "journalistic" feel they have. I think that style contributes to their popularity both by giving a sense of immediacy and of truthfulness. Part of that journalistic feel comes from your choice of language—no swearing, no really sensational descriptions. I hate to use the word "sanitized" but you do seem to take care not to offend, to keep your violence offstage. There is no blatant sex, though characters have affairs and lovers and wives.

Is this avoidance really deliberate, or just a reflection of your own personality? Is it simply that you'd be uncomfortable writing about sex and violence or something else?

TH: It's a combination of things, Ernie. Partly it's a matter of inhibitions, I guess. When I'm writing I'm thinking of my older sister who, I suspect, would be disapproving if I talked dirty. Partly it's a matter of my own feeling that there's no place in the kind of book I write for graphic violence. It destroys the kind of mood I'm trying to build. I don't want to show the reader sadism, extreme suffering, because that would be damaging to the structure of the books.

The same is true of a sex scene. It would be like putting bumps and warts and stuff on the story. Like in architecture when you see a well-designed house and somebody has hung some inappropriate columns on the front porch, see, and they're beautiful but they don't fit the design of the house. Well, that's the way it would be with sex scenes and graphic violence in my books. Actually, it's easy as the dickens to write that stuff.

EB: Most of the writers in the genre are getting more and more graphic these days, so your books have a refreshing quality by avoiding it.

TH: I know my readers tell me it's a relief to be able to read a book without being constantly offended. That kind of stuff has reached the point where it's boring.

EB: I agree. There is another point your readers will not be aware of and that is that traditional Navajos don't swear. Not in Navajo anyway. Curses in Navajo tend to be more like maledictions wishing someone bad luck. They don't have dirty words referring to body parts and functions.

TH: No, they don't seem to have all those euphemisms for anus and penis and all that. I imagine because they didn't have Victorianism imposed on them.

EB: No foolish rules that gave honest objects shock appeal. Without the shock the words lose their fascination.

TH: It all seems perfectly natural, so what's shocking about it? I gather about the worst thing you could say to someone is to call him a coyote.

EB: Or say he has no relatives.

TH: Or that he doesn't take care of his kinfolks. Yeah, that's part of it.

EB: Besides not being appropriate to the style of your books.

TH: I just don't like to write it.

EB: Getting to *A Thief of Time,* where did the original idea for that plot come from?

TH: The stimulus, oddly enough, came from seeing this Bureau of Land Management poster, which pictures a sinister looking fellow with dark glasses and the headline,

"Most of all, I do this creating of scenes while sprawled, apparently comatose, on an old sofa in our living room, or sitting on said sofa

playing a solitaire game
called Spider, which requires two decks
but no imagination.

Thus it is absolutely impossible to tell whether I am writing or loafing.

My wife always gives me the
benefit of the doubt."

"Thief of Time." The message of the poster was obvious—this guy is stealing artifacts, he's stealing our ability to learn about our past and so forth. I saw that and I thought, "Wow, that's a great title for a book."

Actually, the idea for that book had been germinating for some time, years, as a matter of fact. There has been a growing awareness of how much this stealing of artifacts goes on, and awareness of what a big business it is and all the money involved, and the concern of archeologists about it.

It appealed to me as the subject for a book because of the whole business of grave robbing, and I thought it provided such a good way to lead into the different cultures and into the past. That was part of it.

I also enjoyed the irony. It seemed to me the whole business was loaded with irony because the ones so opposed to looting ruins are the world-champion ruin looters—the archaeologists themselves.

When you talk to them, and I talk to a lot of them because they're my friends, they'll tell you the worst looter in the history of the planet was the archaeologist who brought wagons to haul off the artifacts of Chaco Canyon. Even though the stuff went into museums, he wasn't bothering to take proper field notes or anything. They'd string him up today. They'd lynch him if he wasn't already long dead.[*]

What really got the digging going in the Four Corners area was when the University of Utah anthropology department sent word down to the people there that they'd pay five dollars a pot. In the depression years five dollars was a

[*]Richard Wetherill, the man who discovered and first excavated Mesa Verde and other major archaeological sites in the Southwest, had official sanction for his excavation and sale of antiquities from Chaco Canyon. At a couple of international exhibitions in the early years of the century, Weatherill actually had a booth where pottery and other artifacts were offered to the public to finance further work on the ruins. Academics were involved with him at various times.

Other archeologists were known for incredibly sloppy field methods in the early days. The famous Earl Morris apparently never bothered to keep field notes of any kind, nor any documentation of his digs. Such was the state of the discipline well into this century.

week's wages for a hungry man and his family. People were hungry. A starving man could go out with a shovel and dig up two pots and have two week's wages.

EB: As it happens, I know a lot of the people in the antique Indian trade. It's amazing how many of them have degrees in anthropology and archaeology. Several famous people in the business started out digging legally as academics.

TH: So I'm looking at this notion and I'm thinking how much I love the irony. Here's this poor redneck, stealing pots—actually they aren't so poor any more—these ranchers, but few of them are wealthy, and on the other hand [you have] the archaeology people digging up graves. I'd have one of them digging for money, another for prestige— glory in effect—to complete a thesis or get an article published.

EB: You've used that part of the idea before, of course, in *Dance Hall of the Dead,* where the guy was faking an important find. I wonder if readers don't expect academics to be above that kind of thing. It's only a joke that they'd kill to publish. Right?

TH: I'm not so sure. Academics (and I was one for twenty years) in a strange sort of way are highly motivated. I don't know if I was an academic in the sense that I was a scholar, because I was a pretty lousy scholar, but I certainly was surrounded by people who were, and I made my living pretending to be one.

No, they probably wouldn't kill. They tend to be people of thought rather than action but they certainly would destroy one another's reputation and do all sorts of other savage things, and have done them. Very competitive. The literature is full of ferocious, reputation-destroying battles between scholars. Anthropology, certainly has them—academics who would do whatever they could to destroy each other's theories.

EB: In other words, when his career is on the line, an academic can be as tough as anybody else.

TH: As any other line of work, right. In the Early Man field, we had the curator of the Smithsonian Institution who was destroying reputations left and right in defense of his theory that there was no early man in America.

EB: Aleš Hrdlička.*

TH: That went on for years, and woe to the young scholar who ran afoul of him. Anyway, I thought it was a good framework for writing an interesting story and to cast some light on nuances of Navajo culture at the same time.

EB: It also took you into some new territory around Four Corners and the San Juan River.

TH: I hadn't written about that area before, certainly not Chaco.

EB: And as part of the preparation for the book you took a river trip. You like to actually experience the land and places you write about.

TH: For some reason when I'm writing it's essential for me to have in my mind a memory of the landscape, the place where that chapter's action is to take place. So I tend to go around looking for locations like a movie director, for heaven's sake. It might not make much sense, but every writer has to satisfy his own psychological needs, I guess, and that's one of mine.

Anyway, I wanted to find the appropriate places and I floated the San Juan River with the Wild River Expeditions people. I started by asking around about the best way to go and Dan Murphy at the National Park Service told me that

*Aleš Hrdlička, 1869–1943, Bohemian-born physical anthropologist and curator at the National Museum, held that the North American Indians originated in Asia but insisted that an influx could have occurred no earlier than 2000 B.C. His chronology was conclusively refuted in the late 1920s and early 1930s by discoveries near Folsom, Colorado, and Clovis, New Mexico.

a big shot from some junk bond company in New York was lining up a little trip down the San Juan. Murphy was going along as storyteller, and he figured I could hitchhike along.

Sure enough, I found myself in the San Juan canyons where the Anasazi seem to have drifted about the time of the collapse of the big centers at Mesa Verde and Chaco. I was constantly looking for useful stuff as we drifted along, which is what I always do. I can't seem to remember the names of people, but I have a good memory for details, and as I'm drifting down this river I'm seeing things and thinking, "Yes, indeed, that will be part of the book, though I don't know how just yet."

I don't take any notes, just let the impressions stick in the gray matter.

EB: The San Juan country is so beautiful it's almost painful anyway. Gorgeous country.

TH: It really is. It almost seems like another planet when you are down in there, cut off from the rest of the world.

EB: There is a sort of other-worldliness about it.

TH: A wilderness of stone, with all those sloping slanting stratas, which gives you the feeling, though the river isn't moving all that fast, that you are racing down into the bowels of the earth because the land is tilting the wrong way around you.

EB: And geology certainly fits in with your time theme, too. That country literally takes you back to earlier geological periods. An immense move backwards in time.

TH: You find yourself drifting by the very bottom of oil wells—the strange deposits in which the oil pockets formed. A very interesting experience. And the people who ran the trip were so well-informed about the river and its geology, flora, and fauna, which made it much more interesting. Anyway, that was one of the first steps I took to research the book. At the time of the trip the plot was still pretty nebulous in my mind.

EB: So you weren't just looking for locations, you were also looking for inspiration. A visitation of the muse.

TH: It sounds funny to say it, but I was looking for the spirit of the book I suppose.

EB: Certainly the landscape contributes a great deal of the spirit of your books. It is one of the things readers are attracted to.

TH: Something I saw on that San Juan trip eventually caused me to consider the death of Leaphorn's wife, Emma. I saw a heron. A single heron flushed up off an island as we drifted by and he flew downriver into the darkness, and that's how I describe it in the book—how I have Leaphorn see it. But at the time I'm thinking, "One lone heron. What is one lone heron doing here by himself?" He's a migratory bird that mates for life, like swans and geese, and I'm thinking, "Maybe he's a widower."

From there I'm thinking about the bones in my story and I somehow need to personalize those bones that are being dug up. To convert them from artifacts into the remains of real-life mothers and fathers and sons and daughters—human beings that other human beings loved. I needed the notion of having somebody—a principal character involved in personal grief.

EB: That makes sense, of course. One of the things that people who are not fond of the mystery genre are always accusing mystery writers of is being much too superficial. Not having any depth, any real meaning. Again, I think an important aspect of your appeal is that your people are human beings, not superheroes or simple-minded stereotypes.

In Leaphorn you have an older man who is, frankly, almost sad as a character. He's lost his wife, his career is ending, he doesn't have much to live for, much obvious purpose in life. But that defines most people, doesn't it. Leaphorn is still a career professional.

TH: Well, I really think the writer is expecting the reader to suspend his disbelief, believe in murder and so on. So the writer has to let them project that from a base of reality— that is, real people—the kind of people they know and work with and live next to in their daily lives. And a real landscape with real place names.

EB: Your popularity demonstrates that people are anxious to have real people, real human beings as characters, rather than the traditional stereotypical hero.

TH: Well, a lot of readers are, anyway. There are still a lot of mystery readers who read for the puzzle primarily. They want the whodunit, a series of clues and a story in which they engage in this great game with the writer. That's a legitimate expectation, and there is a huge market—the John Dickson Carr-Agatha Christie crowd. It's what made Christie one of the most widely read writers in the world. Frankly, I never liked to read that kind of stuff myself, and I can't write it. But I'd say more than half the readers of mysteries are looking for that, and it bothers them that I don't play the game.

EB: Surely you have enough mystery in your books to keep those readers interested, even though that isn't the central concern of your type of mystery.

TH: I guess sometimes I think I give enough and some-times I don't. Too many of the Agatha Christie readers want to tell me, "I knew who did it right off." And I usually don't care *who* did it, it's *why* it's being done that interests me, or "What's going on here?" is the mystery. I'm con-cerned with motivation, I guess. But all this gives you, as a writer, a tough balancing act to go through.

EB: I don't think you need to stay up nights worrying about it. Your sense of place and character, with your cultural material and unique detectives all seem to serve you well enough. Even your minor characters are intriguing. Where did the idea for the old Mormon come from? Of course the Mormons were the first Anglos to settle in that neck of the woods and the only ones there for a long time.

TH: Again, basing things on reality, that is Mormon country. The important people, the old families, the people who toughed it out and lived there and tamed it and made ranches out of rock gardens were all Mormons. They were important to that area. Most of the early trading families on the Navajo Reservation were Mormon too. And, like everything else, they've been involved with the digging of pots off their own land, off other land probably. It's been in the news some lately.

I needed that character and it seemed logical to base him on the reality of the old Mormon families. It also gave me the chance to take at least a small glimpse of yet another culture. Though you won't learn anything about Mormonism from that book, it gives readers at least the notion that they have a distinct culture of their own that is rooted in that place.

EB: Not much about the religion.

TH: Except maybe how to spell it.

EB: After the Mountain Meadows Massacre, a confrontation between Mormons and some immigrants, the man who took the blame for it all, John Doyle Lee, took refuge in the Colorado River Canyon not far from where your story is set. He hung out there for twenty years in complete isolation. So such a thing could and did happen.

TH: A tough sort of character to live like that, not seeing other people but rarely, living off the land. There was no store to go to. Quite a remarkable bit of American history that's very little known.

One of the frustrations of writing this kind of book is that you are frequently given a situation where you could pull back the curtain and give the readers a bigger peek at something that interests you but you don't feel you can digress into because that's not the story you're writing. So in the interest of plot you just touch on something.

EB: One of the aspects of the book that was a problem for me was the fact that the son, the wild man, had actually committed a pretty atrocious crime, but the father has been protecting him all these years. We need to understand why the father would want to protect him and take care of him all that time. But you are also asking, it seems to me, for the reader to sympathize with him as well. Why did you need to make his crime so horrible?

TH: He had to have committed such an atrocious crime so it wouldn't have been forgotten, so it would have grown and lived on in legend over the years. Something around which a sort of mythology would grow. Something long past but well remembered. Leaphorn sees crime and ugliness every day, but he needed to remember this one crime when the time came.

EB: You think the father could have forgiven him such a crime.

TH: Because he is the father and because he loved his son. I think my books are as much about love as they are about crime. Because the father loved him, he would feel this overwhelming sense of pity. He pitied this child before the terrible events happened, and he couldn't save him. Rage overcame the boy, the disease, schizophrenia, and he killed. But the father loves him still.

EB: Perhaps the novel doesn't give us enough of the past, the crime itself, the motivation.

TH: I didn't give much of that because I supposed readers would know how much fathers love sons.

EB: And it is remote in time at this point.

TH: Facing the fact that Leaphorn isn't a father, I suppose I could have spent more time developing that motivation, but it never occurred to me that I needed it. Now I can see that maybe I did. It might seem unnatural to some people that the father could forgive the boy because the crime was committed against other family members, but fathers tend to concentrate their love on the child who needs it most, the crippled one, the weak link.

EB: Of course, that makes sense.

TH: It makes sense, but looking back on it I should have made all that clearer. Still, when the old man talks about the boy, when he's recalling the past, you sense, I think, that this was his favorite, this was the son, this is where his love was concentrated.

EB: Looking at it that way gives it a Biblical flavor. Tell me about the Reservation evangelist. He was useful in that he could move freely around, but what was he developed from?

TH: I needed someone like that as a source of information. I also, as we've noted, like to explore issues of faith and people of faith, whether they be Mormon or Navajo or Fundamentalist or Roman Catholic or whatever. I was aware of a specific evangelist on the Reservation whom I considered to be self-sacrificing and a man of real faith. I thought I could see how I could use this guy to make the plot move and at the same time plant him as a possible suspect in the readers' minds. You always need plenty of interesting suspects. It also provided another angle on the pottery business. Here's a guy who believes in God, who believes in Christianity, but he's willing to use these pots everyone wants so badly to finance his efforts to bring the Navajos to the Jesus Road, which he believes is the right path. So at least one person is using the pots in an unselfish way.

There is yet another·character, back in New York, who has another use for the pots. I wanted to give a lot of angles on that aspect of the story. So the evangelist functions for me in several ways.

EB: This is almost like the food chain, you know. One little animal eats a smaller animal and is in turn eaten by a larger one. It seems like you had this all worked out in your head.

TH: Not so much, Ernie. As I wrote along, the possibilities kept presenting themselves. Going down that river, for example. At one point we stopped at a place where an early Mormon had built a mill and where another early Mormon had built a trading post and where a trader had been killed in his trading post by a couple of Navajos who fled across the river and disappeared into the Reservation. I kept thinking I could work in the idea of escaping across the river onto the Reservation and disappearing. As it turned out I used it in a much different way, of course. But it stuck in my mind, see, that notion. Originally I came up with another way of doing it that didn't work out.

Further down the river we came to the mouth of Chinle Wash. We stopped there and hiked up the wash to some cliff dwellings. The whole time I was thinking that it would be the perfect location for some of the main action of the book. It was perfect for it. It had all the elements.

I saw the remains of an old sweat bath and thought I had come up with the way to begin the book. I was going to start it with a teenage boy out herding or looking for a horse in that place. He was uneasy because his folks had told him to stay out of that particular canyon, see. I didn't know why at the time, but I figured I would come up with a reason for his discomfort. Some mythology or something. And he would see something frightening, maybe the crime. So that was going to be the first chapter when I started the book.

In fact, I had it open with the kid in the sweat lodge. He's sitting there and hears something outside the sweat bath and he looks out. Then I had a problem with smoke and one thing and another and I dropped that idea. I came up with other ideas, and I kept tinkering around with that kid in the haunted canyon until I could see it wasn't working right and abandoned it.

Anyway, I walked up Chinle Wash and I just kept seeing things I thought I could use. There were all these bats, bats, bats, the prevalence of bats, and I thought, "That's going to be very useful." It wasn't, but I thought it would be.

Then, the first trip down, there had been a big rain somewhere upstream and the potholes were all full of water, though they were diminishing and beginning to dry up. But while there was water all these frogs had hatched out, and I see all these little frogs hopping about. It seemed so incongruous in that desert setting. "The frogs," I thought. "I know I'm gonna use these frogs. Don't know how, but these frogs are going to be in it." Of course the frogs proved to be very useful.

EB: That frog scene at the end of the first chapter of *A Thief of Time* is some of the eeriest writing you've ever done. Most effective. You don't ever really come back and explain those frogs. Except in the obvious sense that the man is completely mad.

TH: It is explained only in Leaphorn's mind when he sees the frogs later and, as you and I would, wonders what in the hell could be going on. He sees it as another evidence of the man's schizophrenia. You can come up with your own conclusion about what he was doing with the frogs. I think that's why I let the reader fill in the blanks.

Here's something of interest to readers who wonder how a book is put together: as I was finishing that first chapter, my original intention was to have the woman walk up on the bad guy actually digging, looting the ruin illegally, and have a confrontation between them. Then I decided I didn't want to do that. I like things like that to happen offstage, off camera, let the reader imagine them. But then I needed a way to end the chapter with something gripping, something that grabs the imagination. I remembered the frogs in the canyon and came up with the business of tethering them because it seemed scary and weird. I figured that as the book developed I'd come up with some way to explain those frogs, the tethered frogs. I hadn't even come up with the crazy man at that point—the guy hiding out in the canyon. That hadn't come to me yet. And the frogs hung there in my mind a long time, looking for an explanation, and that eventually led to the crazy man in the canyon.

EB: In the rough draft I read, you never mentioned the frogs again.

TH: After you told me that, I added the business of Leaphorn seeing the critters and wondering about them.

EB: One thing you've sort of skirted that occurred to me when I first read the manuscript is that it would be impossible for an Anglo—any Anglo—to be anywhere on the Reservation, no matter how remote, without the Navajos knowing about him. He couldn't have been there all those years without being known. Even though he's living in ruins, which Navajos would tend to shun, there would be stories all over the Res about this madman, or ghost, or something.

TH: I never really say they don't know he's there. When

Leaphorn is trying to get the guy to take him to the canyon—the one who'd been digging up the pots—he refused to go there again. He'd seen the chindi ghost, heard him playing the flute, so that is developed in the book, Ernie.

EB: But he would actually be known far and wide. All Navajos would know he existed there and gossip about him, even if they were afraid to chase him away or kill him or something.

TH: Well, the guy who dug the pots does. The reason Leaphorn isn't told about the guy is because this isn't Leaphorn's country—not his stomping grounds. Nobody is going to tell him anything like that without a reason. He's more of a legend than a secret, if I didn't make that clear.

EB: You call this place Watersprinkler Canyon, and the mythological character Watersprinkler is one of at least two Navajo Holy People who is derived in part from the very ancient figure of Kokopelli, who figures importantly in your story elsewhere. How did you happen to come up with the Kokopelli character as a motif in your book? Just because he's a common figure in the rock art?*

TH: That's the main reason. In the San Juan River Canyon he seems to pop up all over the place. Up Chinle Wash I saw him a lot. You see him lying on his back, playing his flute up in the air. Obviously I used that. You see him in various forms—he's very important up that canyon. And he's a figure who provokes the imagination.

EB: Kokopelli combines a lot of characteristics. He is probably an early trickster figure who is also associated with fertility, music, agriculture, and a lot of other things. He is sometimes portrayed with horns, often with a staff of some kind, often with a flute or playing a flute, and usually with

---

*Kokopelli, the humpbacked flute player, is widespread in Southwestern tribal lore, dating far into prehistory as a widely distributed subject of rock art. Depictions of the character range from Alaska to the tip of South America.

a large hunchback. Navajos believe that the hunchback is full of seeds.

TH: The Anasazi probably thought so too. Recently at the Sand Canyon digs they found some new things about Kokopelli. They think now he rose in importance as the protein intake of the people declined. More corn, less meat, and a decline in fertility among the people. As they became less fertile they propitiated Kokopelli.

EB: One thing you don't mention about the figure is that many representations of him show him with a large erection. That is quite a common representation. He is obviously sexual.

TH: I didn't see so many of those in the canyon, but I know that's true.

EB: He obviously fascinated the Navajos because they adapted the hunchback character as a major deity in their own pantheon. You use him partly as a way of identifying this particular pottery in the story.

The idea you advance of being able to follow the work of a single potter has been advanced in recent years as a definite possibility. In fact, I think they've decided now that most of the classic Mimbres pottery was done by perhaps a handful of artists.[*]

TH: That's not where I got the idea, but I saw the Mimbres show at the Museum of New Mexico and I was immensely impressed. The Mimbres work is stunningly beautiful, highly original, and it's obviously very time consuming, creative work by a people who were desperately trying to just stay alive all the time. How did they find time for such art? I don't see how they could have.

*The Mimbres were a prehistoric Puebloan group in southwestern New Mexico. In a relatively short period of time, they produced some of the most striking ceramics ever created. The tribe seems to have come to a sudden and mysterious end around A.D. 1150.

Anyway, when you see the pottery in a large collection it's overpoweringly impressive, which made me think of pottery not as a kind of artifact but as high art. So then I'm thinking, I need some important purpose here that the readers can understand to explain why these archaeologists would work their tails off to get this stuff.

EB: You actually had to have two different lines of pursuit.

TH: Both people couldn't be chasing the same ghost and yet their concerns and searches had to coincide, overlap. I figured if experts could be sure about identifying a person's handwriting, then they should be able to do something like that with pottery. How the shapes were executed, the particular painting, the brushstrokes.

EB: So that was your own idea.

TH: Yes, it was my own. Then I called a specialist down at the University of New Mexico—a person I know and respect—and asked her. She was skeptical, didn't think it was a good idea. But it still hung in my mind. It seemed logical to me, and I thought I didn't want to give it up unless I had to. I'd give it up if it was just plain foolish, of course. So I called another expert and the second one said, "Yes, indeed, some people have already been exploring that, though without much success as yet. But it is a legitimate line of research." A third expert concurred saying, "Yeah, good idea. I think some of that is being done already," and she told me who was working on it. So I said to myself, "OK, two out of three. Let's go with it."

Then I needed a second line of research that would ideally focus on bones. I think about genetics, and I follow much the same process as before. Now I start calling physical anthropologists—the ones involved with skeletons—and from what the first one told me I was already into the writing. Then I talked to someone else who said, "To be really accurate you should have two or three abnormalities you're following to get any solid genetic pattern." Most of the explanation of genetic laws went in one ear and out the other, but I got enough of it to feel like I knew what I was doing. I try to be as authentic and accurate as I can. I revised, revamped, and rewrote according to this new information, and the second line of research focused on this jaw abnormality.

Now the reader had something to follow along. The guy was looking for a certain kind of jawbone, which gave me some nice atmospheric description, too.

Interestingly, I find I have a lot of readers among anthropologists and archaeologists, and I get invited to talk at meetings of these people, like at the Crow Canyon excavations and things like that. They seem to respect the fact that even though I'm not one of them and don't really know all that much I try to be accurate and reflect an accurate sense of what they do, and they never seem to resent the fact that archaeologists are treated rather roughly in my books, you know.

EB: At least two of your major villains now have come from those ranks. Why did you choose St. John's Polychrome as your pottery type, since it is found rather far south of the area you use.

TH: You mean it comes from the wrong part of the Reservation. But some authority suggested it to me in the first place, and someone else told me it was found in various places.

EB: And of course the pottery was traded around to some extent, so it would move from where it originated. I wondered, though, why you didn't just make up a pottery type for your specific needs.

TH: I hate to do that. I wanted to use the name of a real Anasazi pottery type. Maybe that's lazy of me rather than some desire for accuracy.

One of the worst things I did in that book, and I'm going to be embarrassed for the rest of my life for it, was put the Apache Reservation in the wrong place. You didn't catch it either. I know perfectly well where the Mescalero and Jicarilla reservations are. I've spent time on both of them many times. And yet I wrote Mescalero instead of Jicarilla, so I've got the damned Mescaleros where the Jicarillas should be. I fired off a letter to the paperback publishers to make sure they changed it, but it was too late to do anything about the hardcover, which was already in bookstores.

EB: All the more humiliating because you knew better.

TH: Frequently that's the way it is. Your mind just tricks you. I remember in *Ghostway* I've got two guys talking—A said, B said, A said, and then right in the middle I put C said. A guy who's already dead or hadn't been on the scene at all, and it's totally confusing to the reader, I'm sure. Normally, I have good editing for that kind of thing.

EB: I was going to say that catching that kind of error should be part of the editor's job.

TH: It sailed right by the editor and right by me. Pretty weird.

EB: Now for a clever shift of subject on the part of the interviewer. Speaking of plotting problems, didn't you say that the book you're working on now [*Talking God*] had been slow starting, or you had some difficulties with setting up the plot?

TH: Yes, nice transition. I'm still having some problems although the ones I was worrying about when we talked last have been resolved pretty well.

Here's my basic problem: I'm bringing a very rustic story into a very urban area, Washington, D.C., and they simply don't mix well, like oil and water. The Washington plot concerns something rather sophisticated, a struggle between two factions in a South American country. A revolutionary movement against a very cruel, repressive dictatorship. That's fine, but I have to bring my country Navajos into this, me and my country boys. We're involved with a different kind of plot, and I'm finding it difficult to make them mesh.

The story starts out with a Yeibichai and an old Yeibichai mask and a conservator at the Smithsonian who has a Navajo grandmother.* He's flaky and wants to be a Navajo now and is being militant about the return of Native Americans' skeletons, reburial of bones and stuff like that held by museums. He becomes a magnet for two different groups who see ways to use a dissident conservator at a major museum for their own ends. On the one hand we have the South American rebels and on the other a law firm with a peculiar right-of-way problem in New Mexico.

EB: They and your Navajo policemen all come together back in Washington.

TH: Right. But it is hard to make it work. I actually went back there, stayed in the kind of motel that Jim Chee would stay in if he went there. The Smithsonian people were tremendously helpful. They showed me the back rooms and storage bins and the places where my conservator character would likely do his thing and let me watch them at work and gave me a feeling for the system. Took me over to the castle where the big shots have their offices, because one of the characters who appears briefly is a high-ranking fellow at the Smithsonian. But this is all slow work, as it always is. I don't write the books rapidly.

*The Yeibichai (literally "grandfather of the gods," a reference to Talking God), also known as the Night Chant, is a major Navajo wintertime ceremony used to cure blindness, paralysis, migraine, and other serious afflictions. It involves a total of twenty-four masked dancers in addition to numerous sand paintings, prayers, songs, and rites and is performed over an entire week. During a Yeibichai ceremony young people are "initiated" into Navajo religion, new masks are purified, and there is a general blessing for all who attend.

EB: Perhaps that's why your best scenes have the savor of old wine—homemade, of course. There is a richness, a texture about your people and places that suggests a country sense of time and personal integrity. Unlike much of the detective genre, your books are never frantic.

How is it that you haven't written much short fiction—short stories?

TH: Well, they're very difficult for me. You have to develop characters and the setting and get it all done in a single unit, and that's much harder than writing one chapter of a novel. If you don't get it all done, you just write another chapter—pick up where you left off. Condensing an idea isn't comfortable for me. I've only done a few stories and two of those grew out of a letter from *Playboy.*

After I'd won the Edgar award for *Dance Hall of the Dead,* the fiction editor from *Playboy* wrote and asked me to write them a short story. I was delighted because nobody ever liked my stories, and here's somebody actually asking me to write one. So I wrote it and got a wonderful, two-page, very laudatory rejection letter back. But they wanted me to rewrite it. Instead of rewriting it, I wrote another story that brought me a somewhat shorter but still laudatory rejection. I guess they didn't want to offend me. Later I sent one of the stories to an international crime writers competition and it won a prize and a trip to Scandinavia, which was a lot of fun.* But the two stories just sat there. As it turned out, I made two books out of those stories.

EB: Which are?

TH: Actually both stories develop something of the same idea. Jim Chee has been running down some witchcraft gossip and he's been called to Kayenta to talk to an FBI agent. When he gets to the Holiday Inn at Kayenta the agent is waiting for him. Turns out he's a guy Chee had

*Published in this volume as "The Witch, Yazzie, and the Nine of Clubs."

met years before at the FBI academy. The guy is very bright and very ambitious. This fellow has been working on a case involving car thieves—a chain of car thieves. Some gangsters have been hiring people to steal cars on consignment, so to speak. And some of the car thieves in Los Angeles are Navajos. There are supposed to be twenty-five thousand Navajos in LA.

Okay. So the Feds have broken the car ring, and they've gotten some of the big shots and indicted them. They have some of their witnesses on the witness protection program and one of these is a Navajo. They've had the bright idea to hide him on the Reservation, see, like hiding an apple in a barrel of apples.

It works in theory, but they don't take into account that he is a city Navajo not traditionally raised on the Reservation. He's going to stand out like a hideous sore thumb even more than a white man because he doesn't know how to behave like a proper Navajo, see. The FBI agent wants to know how Chee happens to know so much about this guy who's supposed to be a big secret. Chee knows all about him because he's been picking up gossip. Chee, from his side, wants to ask the agent about the witchcraft rumors. He isn't interested, thinks it's all boring superstition. Chee tells him about it anyway.

What it all boils down to, if you know anything about Navajos and Navajo culture as Chee obviously does, is that the protected witness isn't the same man they put there. The assistant district attorney who had been working on the case has quit and gone off—hired away by the organization. The original FBI agent on the case is now dead—killed in a "car accident." So there is no one involved who ever saw the original witness. Of course he's been switched and the original guy murdered. When they get this guy on the witness stand he's going to blow up the whole case. That's the second story and the basis for the novel *Ghostway*.

The other story, which I originally called "Witchcraft Gossip," tried to use the same idea in a different way. The key character in it was a former magician in a carnival side-show, and Chee watches him cheat at a card game, and I use that trick in *The Dark Wind*. When Chee figures out how the trick is done it gives him the solution to the mystery.

EB: That's interesting.

TH: Actually, it works off a kind of intellectual inertia. You get a guy thinking one way and he keeps on thinking that way, even though you reverse the basic situation. It probably wasn't a very good short story, but it grew into a novel, and that happened twice out of that same effort to write a short story for *Playboy*.

EB: They should contact you again. I suppose, then, you don't have plans to try more stories?

TH: They're so tough to write. But I admire good short stories, even if they aren't my forte.

EB: That works both ways. A lot of short story writers were never able to develop a good novel.

As it happens, both of those stories, and virtually all of your novels, have involved witchcraft in some way or another. Witchcraft, the supernatural, skinwalkers and such are all related. Don't you get feedback from readers and critics that perhaps you are exaggerating this aspect of Navajo culture? I know how prevalent these things are, but outsiders must think you overdo it a bit.

TH: I'm sure some of them do, they've said so, and I get that feeling myself sometimes when I'm surrounded by the bright lights of Albuquerque and my Anglo-American cultural assumptions. Then I go onto the Navajo Reservation and get talking to my friends and there it is.

Witchcraft pervades the confounded Reservation and it has a great negative effect on lives and you can't seem to get away from it out there. Some parts are worse than others, and I hear Shiprock is a hotbed of witchcraft.

EB: The area around Piñon, Arizona, is often mentioned in that way. You mentioned something about the ghost lights of Cañoncito.

TH: Cañoncito is a small Navajo reservation closer to Albuquerque. Though a lot of people there claim not to believe in the old "superstitions" as they put it, they have these huge yard lights that burn all night to discourage evil spirits.

One of my Navajo friends who happens to have an MFA degree and is obviously well educated and acculturated, middle-aged, told me that the thing that bothers him most about my books is Leaphorn's skepticism about witchcraft. That doesn't ring true to him as a Navajo. He said, "I've never known a Navajo who was that skeptical about witchcraft." Of course, he would feel like he had to pretend disbelief because of his profession and professional training. I do run into a lot of Navajos who say, "Oh, yeah, I don't believe in that stuff."

EB: Of course, especially if they don't know you very well. They think that's what you want to hear.

TH: But when you get right down to it it isn't true. They do believe. Maybe it's time to use that idea—have a situation where Leaphorn gets involved in such a way that even though he professes not to believe, deep down inside all this time he really does.

EB: I don't really recall that you have given him much deep background in the books, but a man his age would probably have been educated at a mission school. That was what was available for years, along with offreservation boarding schools. All the schools taught Navajos to hide their feelings and beliefs, and he may, as an old-line policeman, come to believe he didn't believe. Intelligent Navajos also realize that witchcraft, no matter how real it might be, is used as an excuse for all kinds of bad behavior and general failures.

TH: In an earlier book I did explain his hostility to the whole idea of witchcraft by going back to an incident that actually happened up in San Juan County. This guy believed that one of his daughters had been made sick, fatally ill, by a witch known to him. He went to the house and killed four "witches" and was tried for murder. I have Leaphorn, as a young cop, hearing about this and, being naturally skeptical, being upset and angry because four innocent people were killed. Five, actually because the father executes himself by committing suicide.

EB: As I said, a mission-educated Navajo might feel he had to persuade himself not to believe in such things, though deep down he really does.

TH: Good thought. I may use it sometime. Leaphorn's deeper cultural feelings. I'll probably remember it. If I do it, Ernie, I'll give you credit.

EB: This witchcraft business, for the record, pervades every aspect of Navajo life. Recently a guy I know bucked off at a rodeo and said, "Well, you know, the reason I bucked off is that my neighbors are jealous of me and witched me." They use witchcraft to explain away all kinds of things to avoid taking blame or responsibility. That was one of the theories of Clyde Kluckhohn when he studied the subject.

TH: In my first book I have an anthropologist writing a book about the use of witchcraft as a social scapegoat.

EB: It makes perfectly good sense to use a traditional explanation to excuse the stress-related behavior of the modern world. Navajos, even those living in pretty remote areas, are subject to a lot of the pressures of the outside world. Getting ahead, making more money, having a new truck, keeping their kids in line. Hardly anyone escapes these days.

TH: A lot of disruptions. That makes sense. It's hard to take all the blame on yourself when things go wrong. You need to find something to focus on, to explain why life is getting so miserable, and witchcraft is handy for a traditional Navajo. It is especially hard to live a good, traditional life in a world that places so much value on pickup trucks and TV sets. Everything is high speed. Navajos run around pretty much the way the general public does.

There is also a tendency on the part of some traditional Navajos to generalize that all the people who leave the Reservation to live in cities are witches.

EB: Because you can't be a proper Navajo outside the boundries of the four sacred mountains.

TH: Right. The book I'm writing now [*Talking God*] doesn't have as much of the Navajo landscape and the Navajo traditions in it as I usually have. That's partly because of the setting and plot, but partly, too, because I have this feeling that my readers have already read all my previous books, and I don't want to repeat myself.

EB: That's probably a fair assessment.

TH: Well, I'm afraid not. Anyway, I have it in my head as a psychological hangup. So I don't want to tell my reader of book nine something I told the reader in book two. I'm afraid he'll say, "Hell, I already know that." It makes it hard, and it probably isn't a good way to write.

EB: Right over your word processor, I see your map of Navajoland so I don't suppose all of the new book is set in Washington.

TH: No, part of it is set down in Lower Greasewood, what

they call the Hopi Buttes, that corner of Red Basin. I have this woman, Agnes Tsosie, who needs a Yeibichai sung over her. That's where part of the story begins. And there's a long chapter east of Gallup along the railroad tracks. I got some help on that from Bernard St. Germain. Do you know him?

EB: He bought a house from me in Gallup.

TH: Small world. I'm planning to write both of you into the book as characters.

EB: That's a fun idea. I'm pleased. Are you feeling pressure, now that you've been on the best-seller list and all, to perform in a certain way. With all this publicity I'm sure your publisher is always pushing on you to get the next book out and all. Then there are the book signings and guest appearances and after-dinner speeches. Is this affecting your writing, your storytelling?

TH: Right now, even as I'm talking to you, my left elbow is resting on the keyboard of my word processor, and I've got this feeling that I should be. . . .

EB: Doing that instead of talking to me?

TH: Writing chapter five. Which should have been written two months ago. On the other hand, I enjoy doing this too.

EB: How is your publisher affecting you? They want you out publicizing the last book, and at the same time they want you here punching out the next one in the series.

TH: There is some of that. One guy from Harper and Row calls me to set up an appearance somewhere, and another one calls from a different department and says, "Tony, I need more details on the new plot because it's gonna be the lead title in the new catalog and we gotta get the cover designed."

EB: So you have to have the new title ready and all of that.

TH: Right, and here I am, thinking "Hell, I got my kids raised and my house is finally paid for. Now I should be able to lay back and go fishing."

EB: I felt that in *Thief of Time* some of the texture was missing, some of your trademark touches, like all the descriptions of sky and clouds and weather. You wrote a whole article about that. Is some of this missing because you're having to work faster, work under pressure?

TH: No, that didn't have anything to do with working faster. I didn't hurry that book at all. It was very slowly written, in fact. I don't let the publisher push me in that way. It had more to do with the season of the year when the book takes place. There isn't as much to describe in the winter on the Colorado Plateau. But it also comes from the feeling that I've done all that before.

We talked about the repetition problem when you write books in a series, and your reader has read all of the earlier books. I'm afraid of repeating myself. Common sense tells me that the readers don't care. In the first place, they probably haven't read all the books and don't remember that well if they did, most of them. Even if they have and do, they probably won't care, as you say. They like that stuff, look forward to it. But I still have that awful feeling that if I repeat myself I'm cheating. I ought to do it the hard way.

EB: But the weather descriptions are a sort of signature— a Hillerman touch, if you will. There is always something new to throw in. How about a flash flood next time? That is a dramatic fact of life on the high plateau. Or a hailstorm. We had a beauty in Gallup last summer.

TH: Or I could bring in a snowstorm, but snowstorms on the Reservation tend not to be all that dramatic. They come in on little cat's feet. Then all of a sudden you're dead.

EB: There are a lot of exposure deaths in the high desert, that's for sure. And I've seen some pretty weird snowstorms, with thunder and lightning and all.

TH: I could describe one of those, when the very front of the squall line bumps up against a warm front. Maybe I'll do that—describe one of those. And lightning in the Southwest is very dramatic.

EB: It violates all the rules. There's the old saying, "Lightning never strikes the same place twice." In the Southwest it always strikes the same place, often over and over again. Navajos have all kinds of taboos regarding lightning-struck objects. Mostly they are negative, but sometimes lightning makes a thing or place holy to medicine men. It is a fearful force in this country.

Back to the signature aspect of this. Has some of this stuff simply become onerous for you? You say, "I'm not going to write about the weather just because you expect me to write about weather."

TH: That's really a good question, Ernie. I've thought about it without coming up with a definitive answer. When I think about it, I'm examining my own conscience, my personal attitude. I think a lot about the details, about the place names being right, things like that. I was careless early on. I moved Burnt Water from one part of the Reservation to another just because I liked the name and wanted to use it. But it was in the wrong place. I never do that any more.

EB: Your geography is generally excellent.

TH: I follow that good old Southern California Auto Club Indian Country map, which is a dandy. I follow it carefully. But I also use my own memory of the landscape. I like to describe the setting, but it should assist the feeling or mood I want to create. Like a feeling of impending disaster, the guy better get a move on or he'll be rained in, that sort of thing. Or use a flash flood to wash out a road. Have the rain come at just the right time to influence the old Hopi. Things like that.

EB: In other words, landscape and weather aren't just furniture, just there for the sake of description. They have to function as well.

TH: That's what my mind tells me. I'm also conscious of the season. Right now, in the new book, they're out by the red cliffs east of Gallup and it's morning. I want the reader to see the red cliffs, you know, and how they look in the morning sun, and I'm trying to visualize what's between the tracks and the distant cliffs. I've seen them plenty of times, and I'm thinking, "You know, I don't remember. I've got to go back and look at that again." The reader couldn't care less.

EB: You could make up anything.

TH: Make up anything. You don't know exactly where the body is found anyway. But you get hung up in those weird problems you impose on yourself that don't really have anything to do with the reader's reaction to the book. It's my own feeling that what I write is true, even though it's fiction. I don't know.

But, no, the book wasn't hurried. It was a very slow book. I didn't meet my deadline on that book, as a matter of fact. First time I've failed to be on time. Actually, I didn't have deadlines in the past, as such. I pride myself on meeting deadlines, but that book just wasn't right. I didn't have it right, and the editor kept asking when they were going to get it, and I kept saying, "As soon as I get it right I'll get it to you, but it isn't right yet." He was understanding. He's an old pro and he knew that certain things can't be hurried. So it wasn't hurried.

EB: The question wasn't so much one of weeks or months, but a general sense of pressure, of expectations perhaps.

As a corollary to that would you say that because of the best-seller list and all expectations are higher? Not just that you have to have a new book each spring, but that each one has to be bigger and better than the one before?

TH: Ernie, that is absolutely nothing new. I have always felt, first and foremost, that I'm a writer. Not a novelist, not a mystery writer, not a journalist. I like to write. I'm a student of writing, and I feel that each thing I do should be better than the last. At least in some way, at least technically, in terms of skill if nothing else. If I can possibly help it, and I *can* help it.

I'm not going to fall into the trap that catches a lot of series writers, of reaching a plateau and then getting steadily worse, just to keep the books coming out on schedule. Sure, the readers will keep buying them for awhile, but I'm not going to do that. I'm going to quit writing rather than write bad books.

EB: A year ago or so you told me you thought maybe you only had one or two more Reservation books in you. Now you're already talking about the next one after the one you're writing—at least you have a basic plot for it. What made you change your mind?

TH: Well, at first I thought how symmetrical it would be if I wrote three Leaphorn books and three Chee mysteries. Then three with Leaphorn and Chee together. That would be enough. But the way my mind works, when I'm starting a book it is the only thing I can think about. As I get closer to finishing it though, I find myself hustling along because I've already got another one waiting to get written. And it's a better one and I want to get started on it, see, and that's the way it's been every time. While I'm in chapter two of the new book I say, "This is it, the last book."

EB: Like while you're writing you get ideas or characters you can't use on the spot, so you start working out a place for them in the next book.

TH: Right. So I can't predict what will happen.

EB: Well, I'm sure your fans will be relieved to hear that you're not killing off Chee and Leaphorn just yet.

THE
WITCH, YAZZIE,
AND THE
NINE OF CLUBS

A

JIM CHEE
MINI-MYSTERY

Tony Hillerman

All summer the witch had been at work on the Rainbow Plateau. It began—although Corporal Jimmy Chee would learn of it only now, at the very last—with the mutilation of the corpse. The rest of it fell pretty much into the pattern of witchcraft gossip one expected in this lonely corner of the Navajo Reservation. Adeline Etcitty's mare had foaled a two-headed colt. Rudolph Bisti's boys lost their best ram while driving their flocks into the high country, and when they found the body werewolf tracks were all around it. The old woman they call Kicks-Her-Horse had actually seen the skinwalker. A man walking down Burnt Water Wash in the twilight had disappeared into a grove of cottonwoods and when the old woman got there, he turned himself into an owl and flew away. The daughter of Rosemary Nakai had seen the witch, too. She shot her .22 rifle at a big dog bothering her horses and the dog turned into a man wearing a wolfskin and she'd run away without seeing what he did.

Corporal Chee heard of the witch now and then and remembered it as he remembered almost everything. But Chee heard less than most because Chee had been assigned to the Tuba City sub-agency and given the Short Mountain territory only six months ago. He came from the Chuska Mountains on the Arizona-New Mexico border three hundred miles away. His born-to clan was the Slow Talking People, and his paternal clan was the Mud Dinee. Here among the barren canyons along the Utah border the clans were the Standing Rock People, the Many Goats, the Tangle Dinee, the Red Forehead Dinee, the Bitter Waters and the Monster People. Here Chee was still a stranger. To a stranger, Navajos talk cautiously of witches.

Which is perhaps why Jim Chee had learned only now, at this very moment, of the mutilation. Or perhaps it was because he had a preoccupation of his own—the odd, frustrating question of where Taylor Yazzie had gone, and what Yazzie had done with the loot from the Burnt Water Trading Post. Whatever the reason he was late in learning, it was the Cowboy who finally told him.

"Everybody knew there was a skinwalker working way last spring," the Cowboy said. "As soon as they found out the witch killed that guy."

Chee had been leaning against the Cowboy's pickup truck. He was looking past the Emerson Nez hogan, through the thin blue haze of piñon smoke which came from its smokehole, watching a half-dozen Nez kinfolks stacking wood for the Girl Dance fire. He was asking himself for the thousandth time what Taylor Yazzie could have done with $40,000 worth of pawn—rings, belt buckles, bracelets, bulky silver concho belts which must weigh, altogether, five hundred pounds. And what had Taylor Yazzie done with himself—another 180 pounds or so, with the bland round face more common among Eastern Navajos than on the Rainbow Plateau, with his thin moustache, with his wire-rimmed sunglasses. Chee had seen Taylor Yazzie only once, the day before he had done the burglary, but since then he had learned him well. Yazzie's world was small, and Yazzie had vanished from it, and since he could hardly speak English there was hardly any place he could go. And just as thoroughly, the silver pawn had vanished from the lives of a hundred families who had turned it over to Ed Yost's trading post to secure their credit until they sold their wool. Through all these thoughts it took a moment for the Cowboy's message to penetrate. When it did, Corporal Chee became very attentive.

"Killed what guy?" Chee asked. Taylor Yazzie, you're dead, he thought. No more mystery.

The Cowboy was sprawled across the front seat of his

truck, fishing a transistor radio out of the glovebox. "You remember," he said. "Back last April. That guy you collected on Piute Mesa."

"Oh," Chee said. He remembered. It had been a miserable day's work and the smell of death had lingered in his carryall for weeks. But that had been in May, not April, and it hadn't looked like a homicide. Just too much booze, too much high-altitude cold. An old story on the Reservation. And John Doe wasn't Taylor Yazzie. The coroner had put the death two months before the body was recovered. Taylor Yazzie was alive, and well, and walking out of Ed Yost's trading post a lot later than that. Chee had been there and seen him. "You see that son-of-a-bitch," Ed Yost had said. "I just fired his ass. Never comes to work, and I think he's been stealing from me." No, Yost didn't want to file a complaint. Nothing he could prove. But the next morning it had been different. Someone with a key had come in the night, and opened the saferoom where the pawn was kept, and took it. Only Yost and Yazzie had access to the keys, and Yazzie had vanished.

"Why you say a witch killed that guy?" Chee asked.

The Cowboy backed out of the pickup cab. The radio didn't work. He shook it, glancing at Chee. His expression was cautious. The bumper stickers plastering the Ford declared him a member of the Native American Rodeo Cowboys' Assn., and proclaimed that Cowboys Make Better Lovers, and that Cowgirls Have More Fun, and recorded the Cowboy's outdated permit to park on the Arizona State University campus. But Cowboy was still a Many Goats Dinee, and Chee had been his friend for just a few months. Uneasiness warred with modern macho.

"They said all the skin was cut off his hands," the Cowboy said. But he said it in a low voice.

"Ah," Chee said. He needed no more explanation. The ingredients of *anti'l*, the "corpse-powder" which skinwalkers make to spread sickness, was known to every Navajo.

They use the skin of their victim which bears the unique imprint of the individual human identity—the skin of palm, and finger-pads, and the balls of the feet. Dried and pulverized with proper ritual, it became the dreaded reverse-negative of the pollen used for curing and blessing. Chee remembered the corpse as he had seen it. Predators and scavenger birds had left a ragged sack of bones and bits of desiccated flesh. No identification and nothing to show it was anything but routine. And that's how it had gone into the books. "Unidentified male. About forty. Probable death by exposure."

"If somebody saw his palms had been skinned, then somebody saw him a hell of a long time before anybody called us about him," Chee said. Nothing unusual in that, either.

"Somebody found him fresh," the Cowboy said. "That's what I heard. One of the Pinto outfit." Cowboy removed the battery from the radio. By trade, Cowboy was the assistant county agricultural agent. He inspected the battery, which looked exactly like all other batteries, with great care. The Cowboy did not want to talk about witch business.

"Any of the Pinto outfit here?" Chee asked.

"Sure," Cowboy said. He made a sweeping gesture, including the scores of pickups, wagons, old sedans occupying the sagebrush flats around the Nez hogans, the dozens of cooking fires smoking in the autumn twilight, the people everywhere. "All the kinfolks come to this. Everybody comes to this."

This was an Enemy Way. This particular Enemy Way had been prescribed, as Chee understood it, to cure Emerson Nez of whatever ailed him so he could walk again with beauty all around him as Changing Woman had taught when she formed the first Navajos. Family duty would require all kinsmen, and clansmen, of Nez to be here, as Cowboy had said, to share in the curing and the blessing. Everybody would be here, especially tonight. Tonight was the sixth night of the ceremonial when the ritual called for the Girl Dance to be held. Its original purpose was metaphysical—part of the prescribed re-enactment of the deeds of the Holy People. But it was also social. Cowboy called it the Navajo substitute for the singles bar, and came to see if he could connect with a new girlfriend. Anthropologists came to study primitive behavior. Whites and Utes and even haughty Hopis came out of curiosity. Bootleggers came to sell illegal whisky. Jim Chee came, in theory, to catch bootleggers. In fact, the elusive, invisible, missing Yazzie drew him. Yazzie and the loot. Sometime, somewhere some of it would have to surface. And when it did, someone would know it. But now to hell with Yazzie and pawn jewelry. He might have an old homicide on his hands. With an unidentified victim and the whole thing six months cold it promised to be as frustrating as the burglary. But he would find some Pinto family members and begin the process.

Cowboy's radio squawked into sudden life and produced the voice of Willie Nelson, singing of abandonment and sorrow. Cowboy turned up the volume.

"Specially everyone would come to this one," Cowboy said toward Chee's departing back. "Nez wasn't the only one bothered by that witch. One way or another it bothered just about everybody on the plateau."

Chee stopped and walked back to the pickup. "You mean Nez was witched?"

"That's what they say," Cowboy said. "Got sick. They took him to the clinic in Tuba City and when that didn't do any good they got themselves a Listener to find out what was wrong with the old man, and he found out Nez had the corpse sickness. He said the witch got on the roof—" (Cowboy paused to point with his lips—a peculiarly Navajo gesture—toward the Nez hogan)—"and dropped *anti'l* down the smokehole."

"Same witch? Same one that did the killing?"

"That's what the Listener said," Cowboy agreed.

Cowboy was full of information tonight, Chee thought. But was it useful? The fire for the Girl Dance had been started now. It cast a red, wavering light which reflected off windshields, faces and the moving forms of people. The pot drums began a halting pattern of sounds which reflected, like the firelight, off the cliffs of the great mesa which sheltered the Nez place. This was the ritual part of the evening. A shaman named Dillon Keeyani was the singer in charge of curing Nez. Chee could see him, a tall, gaunt man standing beyond the fire, chanting the repetitive poetry of this part of the cure. Nez stood beside him, naked to the waist, his face blackened to make him invisible from the ghosts which haunt the night. Why would the Listener have prescribed an Enemy Way? It puzzled Chee. Usually a witch victim was cured with a Prostitution Way, or the proper chants from the Mountain Way were used. The Enemy Way was ordered for witch cases at times, but it was a broad-spectrum antibiotic—used for that multitude of ills caused by exposure to alien ways and alien cultures. Chee's family had held an Enemy Way for him when he had returned from the University of New Mexico, and in those years when Navajos were coming home from the Viet Nam war it was common every winter. But why use it to cure Emerson Nez of the corpse sickness? There was only one answer. Because the witch was an alien—a Ute, a white, a Hopi perhaps. Chee thought about how the Listener would have worked. Long conversations with Nez and those who knew him, hunting for causes of the malaise, for broken taboos, for causes of depression. And then the Listener would have found a quiet place, and listened to what the silence taught him. How would the Listener have known the witch was alien? There was only one way. Chee was suddenly excited. Someone must have seen the witch. Actually seen the man—not in the doubtful moonlight, or a misty evening when a moving shape could be dog or man—but under circumstances that told the witness that the man was not a Navajo.

The Sway Dance had started now. A double line of figures circled the burning pyre, old men and young—even boys too young to have been initiated into the secrets of the Holy People. Among Chee's clans in the Chuskas ritualism was more orthodox and these youngsters would not be allowed to dance until a Yeibichai was held for them, and their eyes had seen through the masks of Black God and Talking God. The fire flared higher as a burning log collapsed with an explosion of sparks. Chee wove through the spectators, asking for Pintos. He found an elderly woman joking with two younger ones. Yes, she was Anna Pinto. Yes, her son had found the body last spring. His name was Walker Pinto. He'd be somewhere playing stick-dice. He was wearing a sweatband. Red.

Chee found the game behind Ed Yost's pickup truck. A lantern on the tailgate provided the light, a saddle blanket spread on the ground was the playing surface. Ed Yost was playing with an elderly round-faced Hopi and four Navajos. Chee recognized Pinto among the watchers by the red sweatband and his mother's description. "Skinny," she'd said. "Bony-faced. Sort of ugly-looking." Although his mother hadn't said it, Walker Pinto was also drunk.

"That's right, man," Pinto said. "I found him. Up there getting the old woman's horses together, and I found him." Wine had slurred Pinto's speech and drowned whatever inhibitions he might have felt about talking of witch business to a man he didn't know. He put his hand on the pickup fender to steady himself and began—Navajo fashion—at the very beginning. He'd married a woman in the Poles Together clan and gone over to Rough Rock to live with her, but she was no good, so this winter he'd come back to his mother's outfit, and his mother had wanted him to go up on Piute Mesa to see about her horses. Pinto described the journey up the mesa with his son, his agile hands acting out the journey. Chee watched the stick-dice game. Yost was good at it. He slammed the four painted wooden pieces down on the base stone in the center of the blanket. They bounced two feet into the air and fell in a neat pattern. He tallied the exposed colors, moved the matchsticks being used as score markers, collected the sticks and passed them to the Hopi in maybe three seconds. Yost had been a magician once, Chee remembered. With a carnival, and his customers had called him Three-Hands. "Bets," Yost said. The Hopi looked at the sticks in his hand, smiling slightly. He threw a crumpled dollar on to the blanket. A middle-aged Navajo wearing wire-rimmed glasses put a folded bill beside it. Two more bills hit the blanket. The lantern light reflected off Wire Rims's lenses and off Yost's bald head.

"About then I heard the truck, way back over the ridge," Pinto was saying. His hands created the ridge and the valley beyond it. "Then the truck it hit something, you see. Bang." Pinto's right hand slammed into his left. "You see, that truck it hit against a rock there. It was turning around in the wash, and the wash is narrow there and it banged up against this rock." Pinto's hands recreated the accident. "I started over there, you see. I walked on over there then to see who it was."

The stick-dice players were listening now; the Hopi's face patient, waiting for the game to resume. The butane lantern made a white light that made Yost's moist eyes sparkle as he looked up at Pinto. There was a pile of bills beside Yost's hand. He took a dollar from it and put it on the blanket without taking his eyes from Pinto.

"But, you see, by the time I got up to the top of the rise, that truck it was driving away. So I went on down there, you see, to find out what had been going on." Pinto's hands re-enacted the journey.

"What kind of truck was it?" Chee asked.

"Already gone," Pinto said. "Bunch of dust hanging in the air, but I didn't see the truck. But when I got down there to the wash, you see, I looked around." Pinto's hands flew here and there, looking around. "There he was, you see, right there shoved under the rabbitbrush." The agile hands disposed of the body. The stick-dice game remained in recess. The Hopi still held the sticks, but he watched Pinto. So did the fat man who sat cross-legged beside him. The lantern light made a point of white in the center of Yost's black pupils. The faces of the Navajo players were rapt, but the Hopi's expression was polite disinterest. The Two-Heart witches of his culture did their evil with more sophistication.

Pinto described what he had seen under the rabbitbrush, his voice wavering with the wine but telling a story often repeated. His agile hands were surer. They showed how the flayed hands of the corpse had lain, where the victim's hat had rolled, how Pinto had searched for traces of the witch, how he had studied the tracks. Behind the stick-dice players the chanting chorus of the Sway Dancers rose and fell. The faint night breeze moved the perfume of burning piñon and the aroma of cedar to Chee's nostrils. The lantern light shone through the rear window of Yost's truck, reflecting from the barrels of the rifles in the gun rack across it. A long-barreled 30.06 and a short saddle carbine, Chee noticed.

"You see, that skinwalker was in a big hurry when he got finished with that body," Pinto was saying. "He backed right over a big chamisa bush and banged that truck all around on the brush and rocks getting it out of there." The hands flew, demonstrating panic.

"But you didn't actually see the truck?" Chee asked.

"Gone," Pinto said. His hands demonstrated the state of goneness.

"Or the witch, either?"

Pinto shook his head. His hands apologized.

On the flat beside the Nez hogan the chanting of the Sway Dance ended with a chorus of shouting. Now the Girl Dance began. Different songs. Different drumbeat. Laughter now, and shouting. The game broke up. Wire Rims folded his blanket. Yost counted his winnings.

"Tell you what I'll do," Yost said to Wire Rims. "I'll show you how I can control your mind."

Wire Rims grinned.

"Yes, I will," Yost said. "I'll plant a thought in your mind and get you to say it."

Wire Rims's grin broadened. "Like what?"

Yost put his hand on the Navajo's shoulder. "Let your mind go blank now," he said. "Don't think about nothing." Yost let ten seconds tick away. He removed the hand. "Now," he said. "It's done. It's in there."

"What?" Wire Rims asked.

"I made you think of a certain card," Yost said. He turned to the spectators, to the Hopi, to Chee. "I always use the same card. Burn it into my mind and keep it there and always use that very same image. That way I can make a stronger impression with it on the other feller's mind." He tapped Wire Rims on the chest with a finger. "He closes his eyes, he sees that certain card."

"Bullshit," Wire Rims said.

"I'll bet you, then," Yost said. "But you got to play fair. You got to name the card you actually see. All right?"

Wire Rims shrugged. "Bullshit. I don't see nothing."

Yost waved his handful of currency. "Yes, you do," Yost insisted. "I got money that says you do. You see the one card I put in your mind. I got $108 here I'll bet you against that belt you're wearing. What's that worth?" It was a belt of heavy conchos hammered out of thick silver. Despite its age and a heavy layer of tarnish it was a beautiful piece of work. Chee guessed it would bring $100 at pawn and sell for maybe $200. But with the skyrocketing price of silver, it might be worth twice that melted down.

"Let's say it would pawn for $300," Yost said. "That gives me three to one odds on the money. But if I'm lying to you, there's just one chance in fifty-two that you'll lose."

"How you going to tell?" Wire Rims asked. "You tell somebody the card in advance?"

"Better than that," Yost said. "I got him here in my pocket sealed up in an envelope. I always use that same card so I keep it sealed up and ready."

"Sealed up in an envelope?" Wire Rims asked.

"That's right," Yost said. He tapped his forefinger to the chest of his khaki bush jacket.

Wire Rims unbuckled the belt and handed it to Chee. "You hold the money," he said. Yost handed Chee the currency.

"I get to refresh your memory," Yost said. He put his hand on the Navajo's shoulder. "You see a whole deck of cards face down on the table. Now, I turn this one on the end here over." Yost's right hand turned over an invisible card and slapped it emphatically on an invisible table. "You see it. You got it in your mind. Now play fair. Tell me the name of the card."

Wire Rims hesitated. "I don't see nothing," he said.

"Come on. Play fair," Yost said. "Name it."

"Nine of clubs," Wire Rims said.

"Here is an honest man," Yost said to Chee and the Hopi and the rest of them. "He named the nine of clubs." While he said it, Yost's left hand had dipped into the left pocket of the bush jacket. Now it fished out an envelope and delivered it to Chee. "Read it and weep," Yost said.

Chee handed the envelope to Wire Rims. It was a small envelope, just a bit bigger than a poker card. Wire Rims tore it open and extracted the card. It was the nine of clubs. Wire Rims looked from card to Yost, disappointment mixed with admiration. "How you do that?"

"I'm a magician," Yost said. He took the belt and the money from Chee. "Any luck on that burglary?" he asked.

"You find that son-of-a-bitch Yazzie yet?"

"Nothing," Chee said.

And then there was a hand on his arm and a pretty face looking up at him. "I've got you," the girl said. She tugged him toward the fire. "You're my partner. Come on, policeman."

"I'd sure like to catch that son-of-a-bitch," Yost said.

The girl danced gracefully. She told Chee she was born to the Standing Rock Dinee and her father was a Bitter Water. With no clan overlap, none of the complex incest taboos of The People prevented their dancing, or whatever else might come to mind. Chee remembered having seen her working behind the registration desk at the Holiday Inn at Shiprock. She was pretty. She was friendly. She was witty. The dance was good. The pot drums tugged at him, and the voices rose in a slightly ribald song about what the old woman and the young man did on the sheepskins away from the firelight. But things nagged at Chee's memory. He wanted to think.

"You don't talk much," the girl said.

"Sorry. Thinking," Chee said.

"But not about me." She frowned at him. "You thinking about arresting somebody?"

"I'm thinking that tomorrow morning when they finish this sing-off with the Scalp Shooting ceremony, they've got to have something to use as the scalp."

The girl shrugged.

"I mean, it has to be something that belonged to the witch. How can they do that unless they know who the witch is? What could it be?"

The girl shrugged again. She was not interested in the subject nor, now, in Jim Chee. "Whyn't you go and ask?" she said. "Big Hat over there is the scalp carrier."

Chee paid his ransom—handing the girl two dollars and then adding two more when the first payment drew a scornful frown. Big Hat was also paying off his partner, with the apparent intention of being immediately recaptured by a plump young woman wearing a wealth of silver necklaces who was waiting at the fringe of the dance. Chee captured him just before the woman did.

"The scalp?" Big Hat asked. "Well, I don't know what you call it. It's a strip of red plastic about this wide," (Big Hat indicated an inch with his fingers) "and maybe half that thick and a foot and a half long."

"What's that got to do with the witch?" Chee asked.

"Broke off the bumper of his truck," Big Hat said. "You know. That strip of rubbery stuff they put on to keep from denting things. It got brittle and some of it broke off."

"At the place where they found the body?"

Big Hat nodded.

"Where you keeping it?" Chee asked. "After you're finished with it tomorrow I'm going to need it." Tomorrow at the final ritual this scalp of the witch would be placed near the Nez hogan. There, after the proper chants were sung, Emerson Nez would attack it with a ceremonial weapon—probably the beak of a raven attached to a stick. Then it would be sprinkled with ashes and shot—probably with a rifle. If all this was properly done, if the minds of all concerned were properly free of lust, anger, avarice—then the witchcraft would be reversed. Emerson Nez would live. The witch would die.

"I got it with my stuff in the tent," Big Hat said. He pointed past the Nez brush arbor. After the ceremony he guessed Chee could have it. Usually anything like that—things touched with witchcraft—would be buried. But he'd ask Dillon Keeyani. Keeyani was the singer. Keeyani was in charge.

And then Jim Chee walked out into the darkness, past the brush arbor and past the little blue nylon tent where Big Hat kept his bedroll and his medicine bundle and what he needed for his role in this seven-day sing. He walked beyond the corral where the Nez outfit kept its horses, out into the sagebrush and the night. He found a rock and sat on it and thought.

While he was dancing he had worked out how Ed Yost had won Wire Rims's belt. A simple matter of illusion and distraction. The easy way it had fooled him made him aware that he must be overlooking other things because of other illusions. But what?

He reviewed what Pinto had told him. Nothing there. He skipped to his own experience with the body. The smell. Checking what was left of the clothing for identification. Moving what was left into the body bag. Hearing the cloth tear. Feeling the bare bone, the rough, dried leather of the boots as he . . .

The boots! Chee slapped both palms against his thighs. The man had his boots on. Why would the witch, the madman, take the skin for corpse powder from the hands and leave the equally essential skin from the feet? He would not, certainly, have replaced the boots. Was the killing not a witch-killing, then? But why the flayed hands? To remove the fingerprints?

Yazzie. Yazzie had a police record. One simple assault. One driving while intoxicated. Printed twice. Identification would have been immediate. But Yazzie was larger than the skinned man, and still alive when the skinned man was dead. John Doe remained John Doe. This only changed John Doe from a random victim to a man whose killer needed to conceal his identity.

The air moved against Chee's face and with the faint breeze came the sound of the pot drums and of laughter. Much closer he heard the fluting cry of a hunting owl. He saw the owl now, a gray shape gliding in the starlight just above the sage, hunting, as Chee's mind hunted, something which eluded it. Something, Chee's instinct told him, as obvious as the nine of clubs.

But what? Chee thought of how adroitly Yost had manipulated Wire Rims into the bet, and into the illusion. Overestimating the value of the man's belt. Causing them all to think of a single specific card, sealed in a single specific envelope, waiting to be specifically named. He smiled slightly, appreciating the cleverness.

The smile lingered, abruptly disappeared, reappeared and suddenly converted itself into an exultant shout of laughter. Jim Chee had found another illusion. In this one, he had been Yost's target. He'd been totally fooled. Yazzie *was* John Doe. Yost had killed him, removed the fingerprints, put the body where it would be found. Then he had performed his magic. Cleverly. Taking advantage of the circumstances—a new policeman who'd never seen Yazzie. Chee recreated the day. The note to call Yost. Yost wanting to see him, suggesting two in the afternoon. Chee had been a few minutes late. The big, round-faced Navajo stalking out of Yost's office. Yost's charade of indignant anger. Who was this ersatz "Yazzie"? The only requirement would be a Navajo from another part of the Reservation, whom Chee wouldn't be likely to see again soon. Clever!

That reminded him that he had no time for this now. He stopped at his own vehicle for his flashlight and then checked Yost's truck. Typical of trucks which live out their lives on the rocky tracks of the Reservation, it was battered, scraped and dented. The entire plastic padding strip was missing from the front bumper. From the back one, a piece was missing. About eighteen inches long. What was left fit Big Hat's description of the scalp. His deduction confirmed, Chee stood behind the truck, thinking.

Had Yost disposed of Yazzie to cover up the faked burglary? Or had Yazzie been killed for some unknown motive and the illusion of burglary created to explain his disappearance? Chee decided he preferred the first theory. For months before the crime the price of silver had been skyrocketing, moving from about five dollars an ounce to at least forty dollars. It bothered Yost to know that as soon as they sold their wool, his customers would be paying off their debts and walking away with that sudden wealth.

The Girl Dance had ended now. The drums were quiet. The fire had burned down. People were drifting past him through the darkness on their way back to their bedrolls. Tomorrow at dawn there would be the final sand-painting on the floor of the Nez hogan; Nez would drink the ritual emetic and just as the sun rose would vomit out the sickness. Then the Scalp Shooting would be held. A strip of red plastic molding would be shot and a witch would, eventually, die. Would Yost stay for the finish? And how would he react when he saw the plastic molding?

A split second into that thought, it was followed by another. Yost had heard what Pinto had said. Yost would know this form of the Enemy Way required a ceremonial scalp. Yost wouldn't wait to find out what it was.

Chee snapped on the flashlight. Through the back window of Yost's pickup he saw that the rifle rack now held only the 30.06. The carbine was gone.

Chee ran as fast as the darkness allowed, dodging trucks, wagons, people and camping paraphernalia, toward the tent of Big Hat. Just past the brush arbor he stopped. A light was visible through the taut blue nylon. It moved.

Chee walked toward the tent, quietly now, bringing his labored breathing under control. Through the opening he could see Big Hat's bedroll and the motionless outflung arm of someone wearing a flannel shirt. Chee moved directly in front of the tent door. He had his pistol cocked now. Yost was squatting against the back wall of the tent, illuminated by a battery lantern, sorting through the contents of a blue cloth zipper bag. Big Hat sprawled face down just inside the tent, his hat beside his shoulder. Yost's carbine was across his legs . . .

"Yost," Chee said. "Drop the carbine and . . ."

Yost turned on his heels, swinging the carbine.

Jim Chee, who had never shot anyone, who thought he would never shoot another human, shot Yost through the chest.

Big Hat was dead, the side of his skull dented. Yost had neither pulse nor any sign of breath. Chee fished in the pockets of his bush jacket and retrieved the concho belt. He'd return it to Wire Rims. In the pocket with it were small sealed envelopes. Thirteen of them. Chee opened the first one. The Ace of Hearts. Had Wire Rims guessed the five of hearts, Yost would have handed him the fifth envelope from his pocket. Chee's bullet had gone through the left breast pocket of Yost's jacket—puncturing diamonds or spades.

Behind him Chee could hear the sounds of shouting, of running feet, people gathering at the tent flap. Cowboy was there, staring in at him. "What happened?" Cowboy said.

And Chee said, "The witch is dead."

BIOGRAPHIES

TONY HILLERMAN

In a country where successful authors love to assert their humble origins, Tony Hillerman has little need to boast. Coming of age in World War II, Tony's childhood embraced the Depression from the heart of Steinbeck's Oklahoma dust bowl. "The difference between the Joads and the people around Sacred Heart," he says, "was that the Joads had enough money to buy gasoline to get to Shawnee. The area's claim to fame lay in its designation as the region most critically affected by soil erosion in the United States.

Ironically Oklahoma had been wilderness only a generation before, given to the Indians as land with no possible future economic value. Then, with the continuing demand for new land, the Territory was opened for the last great land rush. While most of the area filled with Bible-thumping fundamentalists from the deep South, Sacred Heart became a tiny island of German- and French-named Catholicis. The nucleus of the tiny village was a country store Hillerman's dad owned with a partner. There was also a cotton gin and a filling station, though the land now grew little cotton. On the hill was the Catholic church and below the hill was a monastery, already largely abandoned, and a boarding school.

The Sisters of Mercy had built a school for Pottawatomie Indian girls and allowed a handful of the farmboys to attend for a modest tuition, though the boys were never allowed to play with the girls. In the only other school one teacher taught eight grades in two rooms, a common enough situation at the time. After the eighth grade as a day student in the girls' school Tony rode a bus to Konawa to attend school with the "city" kids.

Years later Hillerman realized that the town boys were almost as bumpkinish as he, but at the time they seemed devilishly wise and sophisticated. "There probably wasn't anyone in Konawa that wasn't below the current poverty level," recalls Tony, "except maybe the banker and the town doctor." He remembers the time a neighbor sent one of the kids next door, a mile-and-a-half walk, to borrow enough cash money for a postage stamp. "A stamp was three cents then. We had the three cents."

Growing up with an older brother and sister, Tony recalls childhood as a happy time. They had plenty to eat, and though the farmwork was demanding and money scarce there were the benefits of a slow and even lifestyle, country values, and what seemed like unlimited countryside to play in. "And we loved to read." Though the state library was somewhat eccentric in the books they passed on to him, he didn't care. "Hell, we'd read anything on paper. I'll still read anything."

Another source of books was the abandoned monastery. When the order moved to the county seat and built a college, they left a lot of books behind—damaged copies, duplicates, and books in German, French, and Latin. At the age of twelve Tony talked the parish priest into letting him catalog this curious collection with his brother. He was soon conversant with Plutarch, the complete works of Washington Irving, and Prescott's *Conquest of Mexico*.

Tony particularly recalls the blood and guts gore of "*The Lives of the Saints*, about all those people being burned at the stake, having their fingernails pulled out, having their eyelids cut off, and all the gruesome ways the martyrs got martyred." He also remembers some early mysteries he read, including Chesterton and Mary Roberts Rinehart. But it was the aborigine detective of Australian writer Arthur Upfield who really impressed him.

Though Tony had been a good student, graduating from high school at sixteen, he hadn't thought of going to college. "Nobody from Konawa ever went to college." His father died the Christmas after Pearl Harbor, the victim of a heart condition. "He literally worked himself to death between the store and the farm." One evening, sitting around the kitchen table, his mother and older brother decided to send him off to college. "So I was sent off to Oklahoma State. We didn't even know when school started, except that it started in the fall."

School had already been going for ten days when he got there, and his hastily appointed advisor shoved him into some classes. The family had just enough money to pay his small tuition, buy most of his books, and pay his first month's rent. After that he was on his own. He got a dishwashing job that provided meals but no money and ended up with three other part-time jobs. "We found this condemned two-storey building run by this old lady as a boarding house. I got half a room with one double for $7.50 a month. I had to share the bed with a guy from Oklahoma City."

Even with four jobs Hillerman couldn't make enough to cover his second semester in college, which actually came as something of a relief. Older brother Barney had enlisted and gone off to fight, leaving the Hillerman farm and other affairs for the still teenaged Tony. Within a year he joined the army, sold off the livestock, the team of horses, and locked up the old home place. "I was eighteen and scared to death the War would end before I could get in it. I was a war lover. It wasn't just good and bad, a fight against evil. I was just plain fascinated by war. When I went into the infantry I could name every Italian tank, armament, which kind of grenades they issued German paratroopers, and the operating range of a Fiat. I was crazy about that sort of stuff. I knew exactly how many destroyers the German navy had."

Since Hillerman had scored very high on his entrance exams, the military shunted him into something called the Army Specialized Training Corps. In Tony's case they sent him right back to the college he'd just quit. "That only lasted a couple of months, and the army said to hell with this idea and dumped us all in a rifle company." This group of best and brightest was suddenly cannon fodder in the 103rd Division.

Tony shipped overseas in September 1944 and was seriously wounded the following February. Of the 212 men who had arrived in France with him only thirty-two were then left. A medic told him later he had appeared to be a goner. Wounded in the head and with both legs broken, they had left him to die or be treated by the doctors from the battalion.

"While we were recovering in the hospital I took part in the world's greatest, longest, Guinness-Book-of-Records poker game," he recalls proudly. "It went on nonstop for months and months, and it was held on my bed because I was in a body cast and couldn't move. When Roosevelt died I was on crutches and most of the other guys were also mobile by then, and the head nurse came by to tell us they were going to have a memorial service for the late President. We told her we'd have a moment of silent prayer. She got so pissed off that we wouldn't go to the memorial service that she took our cards away from us and ended the game."

While Army stories are not part of the Hillerman repertoire, six months of fighting earned him a Bronze Star, a Silver Star, and a Purple Heart. Returning to the States in 1945, he used a telephone line for the first time in his life to call his mother from a hospital in New York. Since the farm had been pretty well disposed of when Tony left home, and he had his GI Bill benefits, returning to college was the obvious next step.

Because of his wartime decorations the *Daily Oklahoman* had done an article on Hillerman. The woman who wrote the piece had borrowed Tony's letters home from his mother and was so impressed by his writing ability that she asked to see him when he got home. "I went to see her and she told me I ought to be a writer. Hell, I knew I wasn't going to be an engineer because I knew how bad I was in math and didn't like it anyway. So I thought, why not?" Thus a career in journalism and writing was born.

He met Marie Unzner when they were both seniors, and they married in 1948. As Tony delights to tell, his first job was writing commercials for Purina Pig Chow and Cain's Better Coffee, a job he claims to have hated. At the time he simply couldn't find a job as a reporter. He finally landed a stint with the *News Herald* in Borger, Texas, north of Amarillo. Soon after that he joined some friends in a little paper in Lawton, Oklahoma. From a job with United Press International he was offered the post of bureau chief in Santa Fe, New Mexico, in 1952. He recalls leaping at the chance, adding, "I have always wanted, since I started in journalism, to be the editor of a state capitol newspaper. I made it, but it was back-breaking work. I rarely even had a Sunday off." From political reporter in 1954 to city editor to managing editor and finally executive editor, Hillerman stayed with the *New Mexican* until 1962, winning several writing awards along the way.

Few men in their late thirties, in the midst of successful careers and with a wife and five kids, suddenly undertake major life changes, but Tony visualized returning to school and getting paid to do it. Among other things, he wanted to try another kind of writing—maybe pen the Great American Novel or something. Of course he was known to the journalism department at the University of New Mexico and the department head, Keen Rafferty, told him the English department was pretty good. "Tom Popejoy thinks a lot of you," he added. Hillerman had supported President Popejoy in a fight with right-wingers and the American Legion. They made an appointment and Tony found himself with a job as assistant to the President of the University of New Mexico—a sort of ambassador without portfolio. In the early sixties the school was growing by leaps and bounds and new problems sprang from everywhere. For several years Tony was a troubleshooter for the school. He wrote proposals, traveled to Washington, scrounged mattresses for the sheriff's department, and worked on a land grant for the school. Once, "I went down to Ecuador with a big fat envelope full of money to get two UNM students out of prison."

In the meantime Hillerman was enrolled as a student, initially on nondegree status to make up deficiencies. He went on to become a professor and then head of the Journalism department. And as if that wasn't more than enough for one person, he was working away at writing the novel. "A guy named Morris Friedman taught me a lot. He was the head of the English department for a time. He detected right away that I never wrote in the first person and had a hangup about it. He forced me to write in the first person, and it made a lot of changes in me and the way I write. He was a good teacher. He knew how to reinforce your strengths and point out your weaknesses."

All of which eventually led to the publication of *The Blessing Way* in 1970 and the long string of novels and awards that have followed in the two decades since. Tony and Marie are finally building a new house in the North Valley of Albuquerque, but Tony says the only special feature will be a really big office. This is one man who remains unspoiled by success. Only last year did he finally get an unlisted telephone number, because Marie was having to field dozens of silly phone calls a day. He is well into new books featuring Leaphorn and Chee, though arthritis curtailed his promotional activities somewhat. He still plays poker once a week with his old cronies, and he still finds time for old friends, thank goodness.

ERNIE BULOW

E rnie Bulow is a sometime bookman whose interests and experience extend to journalism, photography, Indian trading, writing, silversmithing, and teaching. He claims he could probably make a decent living as a trader, if he didn't have so much fun at it. As it is, he continues to include a few traders among his friends, despite his better judgment.

Born in San Francisco in 1943, Bulow first encountered some of the Navajo people while working alongside the migrant laborers on his grandfather's farm in southern Idaho. After taking a degree in English in the early sixties, he worked for the Bureau of Indian Affairs, living in Gallup and teaching English at Fort Wingate on the Navajo Reservation. During this time he saw or took part in all the major Navajo healing rites.

Following receipt of a doctorate from the University of Utah, he returned to New Mexico, where he traded in Indian jewelry and kachinas and opened a bookstore, among other activities. Currently he writes reviews for the *Gallup Independent,* teaches an occasional class at the Gallup branch of the University of New Mexico, and deals in rare books.

ERNEST FRANKLIN

Born in 1943, Ernest Franklin is a Navajo from Twin Lakes, New Mexico, on the "Big Reservation." His first language was Navajo, and he grew up familiar with horses, guns, hard work, and the desert landscape of the Southwest. He spent his high school years at the now defunct Albuquerque Indian School and later served a three-year stint in Viet Nam.

Franklin has had a longtime love affair with the rodeo and still enters the "old-timers" events held at many Reservation shows. He continues to keep a small flock of sheep because, "What's a Navajo without a sheep herd?"

Rodeo is also a favorite subject for his painting, and Franklin considers himself more a cowboy artist than an "Indian" painter. Though he began drawing at an early age, his formal art training has been sporadic but includes workshop grants from the Rockefeller Foundation and studies at Fort Lewis College and the University of New Mexico.

His work, some of which follows, has appeared in four one-man shows and many group exhibitions in the Southwest. He has been illustrating the Hillerman characters for several years, and Tony recently inscribed a presentation copy of *Talking God,* "For my friend Ernie Franklin. Thanks for showing me what Chee and Leaphorn look like."

AFTERWORD

Taking a new look at *Talking Mysteries* was a mind-boggling way to remind myself of how fast the years fly by. When Ernie Bulow and I were having the conversation which gave *Talking* its title, I was struggling to patch together a plot for my "Next Book." I had an accumulation of ideas waiting to get into a book, including the notion of using memories of the historic border warfare raiding between Navajos and Utes—a somewhat more civilized version of what now goes on between Israel and Palestine. One notion was to create a fictional robbery of the Ute Mountain Casino, and another was to somehow work in the old coal mining activities of Mormon settlers in the Bluff area. And then I was yearning to do something with the U.S. Environmental Protection Agency's efforts to locate the hundreds of abandoned uranium digs in that part of the Navajo Reservation. Those ideas bumped together with a dozen or so more, finally reached the critical mass needed for fusion, and "Next Book" became *Hunting Badger*.

Today, a dozen years later, I am facing exactly the same problem—in other words, older but no wiser. Now the "Next Book" will concern that catastrophic collision of two airlines over the Grand Canyon in 1956, which killed everyone aboard both of them and sent bodies showering down the cliffs and into the Colorado. It was the worst aircraft disaster in history at the time, and I intend to add a fictional diamond dealer to its list of victims and spin a yarn involving Navajos, Hopis, and the tribes who occupy the canyon and its rims.

Someday Ernie and I both plan to retire. But not yet.

Tony Hillerman
November 2003

Books by Tony Hillerman

FICTION

The Blessing Way (1970)

The Fly on the Wall (1971)

The Boy Who Made Dragonfly (1972)

Dance Hall of the Dead (1973)

Listening Woman (1978)

People of Darkness (1980)

The Dark Wind (1982)

The Ghostway (1984)

Skinwalkers (1986)

A Thief of Time (1988)

Talking God (1989)

Coyote Waits (1990)

Sacred Clowns (1991)

Finding Moon (1993)

The Fallen Man (1994)

The First Eagle (1995)

Hunting Badger (1997)

The Wailing Wind (1999)

Buster Coyote (for children) (2000)

The Sinister Pig (2002)

NONFICTION

The Great Taos Bank Robbery (1973)

New Mexico (1974)

Rio Grande (1975)

The Spell of New Mexico (1976)

Indian Country (1987)

Hillerman Country (1991)

The Best American Mystery Stories
(with Otto Penzler) (1997)

The American Detective Story
(with Rosemary Herbert) (1998)

Seldom Disappointed (2001)